THE MATH OF SUCCESS

The Building Block Method To Create A Life You Can Count On!

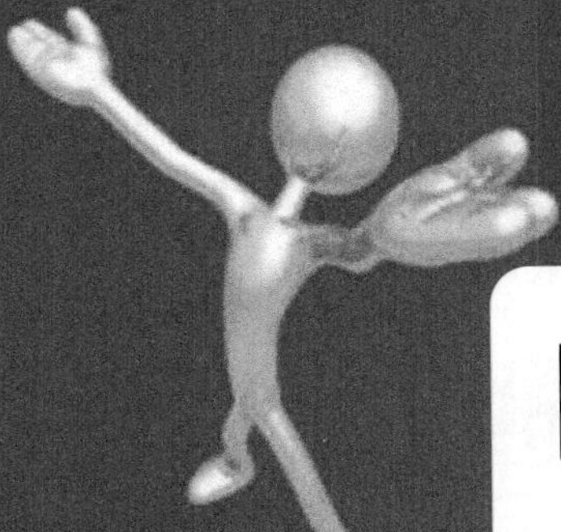

DR. MARK ZUPO

THE MATH OF SUCCESS

The Building Block Method To Create A Life You Can Count On!

DR. MARK ZUPO

THE MATH

OF

SUCCESS

USE YOU KNOWLEDGE, EDUCATION AND EXPERIENCE TO BUILD MULTIPLE STREAMS OF INCOME

THE MATH OF SUCCESS

The Building Block Method
of Creating a Life You Can Count On!

By

Dr. Mark Zupo

The Math of Success!
The Building Block Method of Creating a Life You Can Count On

Published by Slippery Rock Press Publishing™, Atlanta, GA.

For additional information on products, services or coaching, go to:
www.MarkZupo.com

ISBN-10: 0-9964000-0-1

ISBN-13: 978-0-9964000-0-8 (Mark Zupo)

Also available in audio / CD / eBook / Kindle™ formats

Printed in the Unites States of America

THE MATH OF SUCCESS™

The Building Block Method of Creating a Life You Can Count On!

By Dr. Mark Zupo

1205 Johnson Ferry Road, Suite 136-116
Marietta, Georgia 30068
Published by
Slippery Rock Press Publishing™, LLC.
Mark Zupo International, LLC.

ISBN-10: 0-9964000-0-1
ISBN-13: 978-0-9964000-0-8 (Mark Zupo)

Printed in the United States of America.

10 9 8 7 6 5 4 3 2 1

(I have no idea why these numbers are here.
But they make my book look good, so I included them too.)

The Math

OF

SUCCESS

USE YOU KNOWLEDGE, EDUCATION AND EXPERIENCE TO BUILD MULTIPLE STREAMS OF INCOME

DR. MARK ZUPO

DEDICATION

I dedicate this book to my children, Traci, Matthew, Chris and Kate. As of today, Matthew, Chris and Kate are young and do not have the comprehensive ability to use what I teach in this book. My hope is that after I am gone, they will find it, read it and use as the tool for their eventual entrepreneurial business and life successes.

"There is no better example of failure than me.
But, there is no better illustration of
triumph over tragedy than me too."

- Dr. Mark Zupo

Success can be proven.

Divide workload and skill among those more talented.

Subtract negativity and doubt from your resolve to achieve.

Add energy and enthusiasm to the direction and determination.

Multiply your efforts by sharing workload, success, experience, and passion.

These laws of success are universal, unwavering, calculable, and reliable and established in the origins of proof.

Follow these rules and failure will be an afterthought.

- Dr. Mark Zupo

Table Of Contents

Your Opportunity To Change Your Life!....1

Forethought....2

Table Of Contents....2

ACKNOWLEDGMENTS....15

INSIGHTS....16

PART 1 The Blueprint....19

PART 2 The Formula....19

PART 3 The Action Steps....19

PART 1....22

The Blueprint....22

Module 1....23

10 Traits of Explorers....23

Module 2....32

WHY IS HE RICH AND I'M NOT?....32

Module 3....45

Wealthy or Rich Formulas....45

Module 4 54

7 Important Lessons I learned From My Failures 54

PART 2 61

The Formula 61

Module 5 62

Guaranteed Opportunity 62

Module 6 70

My Failure Resume 70

The Magic of 100 75

Module 7 85

The Multiple Streams Mastery System™ 85

***NOTE - This is my best predictable revenue generator EVER!** 88

MULTIPLE STREAMS MASTERY™ 92

PART 3 96

The Action Steps 96

MODULE 8 My Stream Runs Up Hill! 97

The Magic of Multiple Streams of Income 97

Multiple Streams Mastery™ Rolled Into One Amazing Opportunity. 97

Module 9 104

MODULE 10 114

See It to Believe It....114

"What would ~~you~~ I do if ~~you~~ I had start all over again?" 121

Part 4....128

The Opportunity 128

MODULE 11 129

Building an Online Business With Multiple Streams of Income™ 129

Charge on and make it happen! 141

MODULE 12 WHAT IF?....143

MODULE 13 154

HOW TO FAIL SUCCESSFULLY 154

MODULE 14 160

IT'S ALL GONE!....160

THE BIG PICTURE 163

The lesson here is: Relationship-Building 163

MODULE 15 172

CALL TO ACTION 172

Resources 235

Appendix 2 237

Internet Business Tools I Use 237

Upcoming Projects 238

BookKamp™ 238

MPI™ The Passive-Profits Mastery Program ™ for aspiring entrepreneurs to build a brand and a business that is recognized immediately. 238

Appendix 3 239

Systems 239

ABOUT THE AUTHOR 244

Business-Building Diagrams™ 247

Your Opportunity to Change Your Life!

Next Steps....YOUR FREEDOM REVOLUTION
Creating Your Personal Success Movement

"Freedom is a wonderful thing. It is only restricted by everyone

else who determines the degree of freedom we may enjoy."
- Dr. Mark Zupo

Forethought

What This Book is About

Hello, I am Dr. Mark Zupo...

There are plenty of great books for you to choose from. But, many people find one incredible book that completely changed their purpose, direction, and their life. This book represents many years of hard work and many illustrations of some of my greatest failures. However, the summation represents my greatest achievements. This book is more about the platform for what I believe to be huge when it comes to earning the privilege to be a success, whatever success may be for you too.

I firmly believe that my success was as emotional as my losses were too. Success could not have been as sweet as they are unless it cost along the way. That cost is the value we will talk about in more depth later.

Pursue your passions like there is no tomorrow.

To begin, ask yourself, "Are you pursuing your dreams with all the passion you have or just along for the ride on a life you do not control?" This question begs the answer that you are not only chasing your dreams but catching them and living your life by your design! Let's examine both options and choose the one right for you.

A Life by Design or Default

There are four foundations of emotional success I hold firmly as the guide that allowed me to believe in myself and forge ahead under great scrutiny and criticism.

- ✓ LOVE: This is the primary of all emotional characteristics that will keep you in friendship and relationships. Companionship and camaraderie that is meaningful and with purpose.
- ✓ GREED: As much as it defiles our sense of duty and responsibility, it is like the germs in your gut has a role to play in our desires, wants and needs. Natural or not, without a tinge of greed we fail to want, desire and need.
- ✓ DUTY: The responsibility we face is the engine that drives our obligation to prove, produce and provide for those we love. Honor, the greatest of our duties is at the front of our sense of accomplishments.
- ✓ FEAR: Our primal response to charge ahead considering impending doom or loss can make heroes of us all. Given the time, the opportunity and the need, fear can be the greatest of motivators to act against loss, failure and danger.

These traits are what drive me, and I predict that they can be the driving force in your life too when appropriate. This book exists because I was a failure at mathematics from the start. I hated math, I avoided it and flunked it many times. My challenge was to embrace it and conquer it if I was ever to find success in it. That said, this is the proof that I have made it work for me as I believe using simple math can work for you.

P.S. It isn't complicated, I promise.

First, we must examine and define what a life by design is and then find the difference to the life by default. To better understand the options, we must look at where we are now and where we have come from.

If you feel that your life is passing us by basically because we recognize that the many things that we wanted to do and want out of life are not there or just have not happened. Am I right? The answer lies in our ability to compromise. It is the easiest talent we all share next to procrastination.

As we grow older we realize that the value of time is a commodity that is smaller and smaller as every day goes by. We also realize the value of the time we have lost as the days went by. Many of us experience the same opportunity for challenge.

How we deal with them individually is the key to whether we realize the success we dream of or whether we experience the failures we hear of.

We can make a parallel of the days we lose in our life to the Earth. Yes, really. We routinely go throughout the day never paying much attention to the Earth's rotation around the sun. Yet we use it to guide our life every moment of the day, don't we?

The sun comes up, we eat breakfast (or not if we are running late…lol), dress and leave for work. We spend the day working at our jobs and look to the clock for the time. The Earth rotates and delivers dawn, daylight, mid-day, dusk and night. ...and everyone on the planet has the same time and path that not all of us take advantage of at the time. There are a few conditions that determine your life successes.

Here Are 10 Unique Attributes That Support Success.

Attribute 1. *Give Yourself Permission*

The first task to develop a fully engaged success plan for your life is to give yourself consent to be a success regardless of what others think, say or do. Give yourself permission to succeed. Sounds a bit "korny" but the impact on your mindset is astounding!

Your success is undeniable, irrevocable and unbelievable. See it, believe it and act on it.

Attribute 2. Be *Passionate*

My Mother is the most generous and wonderful human being I have ever known. She is also the greatest example of "sales through guilt!" Her passion knows no bounds. My Mother is 85, still works every day and is as enthusiastic about life as she ever was. That's passion.

Attribute 3. *Believe in Yourself*

Self-belief is the confidence in your own judgment, skills and abilities. To live a successful life, it is imperative that you believe in yourself unconditionally. Self-belief is your willingness to never quit. It is your willingness to rebound from every obstacle or failure in the pursuit of your dreams. I earned a doctorate at 62 years old. Once people commit to a belief, the strength of the belief is fortified by their ability to defend it. There is no accepted "norm" when we think of a doctorate student and age or experience doesn't matter. I believed in myself – this is POWER!

"It's never too far.
It's never too late.
You're never too old."

- Dr. Mark Zupo

Attribute 4. Be *Adventurous*

Part of the definition of adventure is, "...something that must happen..." An adventure in success is then defined as *"something that must happen!"* Can you deny that your success is eventually guaranteed? Wikipedia defines adventure as, "...an exciting or unusual experience. It may also be a bold, usually risky undertaking, with an uncertain outcome. Adventures may be activities with some potential for physical danger such as traveling, exploring, skydiving, mountain climbing, scuba diving, river rafting or participating in extreme sports.

The term also broadly refers to any enterprise that is potentially fraught with physical, financial or psychological risk, such as a business venture, or other major life undertakings.

Embrace your success as an adventure.

"One of the hardest things for people to do is
not to recognize their passion but to pursue it.

-Dr. Mark Zupo

Attribute 5. Apply *Reason to Your Beliefs*

Reason is the capacity for consciously making sense of things, applying logic, establishing and verifying facts, and changing or justifying practices, institutions, and beliefs based on new or existing information. I have often said, if you understood the impact of a single positive thought could have on your life you would never think a negative thought again!"

Attribute 6. *Be Generous*

If you want to be happy, practice generosity. If you want to help others to be happy, practice generosity. If you expect success, then expect to be generous in other's success. "The quality of being kind and understanding, the willingness to give other people things that have value defined as an act of selflessness." Show the depth of your generosity by displaying the genuineness of intent.

Attribute 7. Be *Curious*

The quality of exploring the unknown or something strange or fascinating. Surely, any form of business starts here! Especially an online Internet-based business. Never fear, it is just one discovery that you will make to achieve your goal of success. Be curious. Be an adventurer. Charge ahead and discover your most prized opportunities that lay in wait for you to find. ***Success.***

Attribute 8. *Project Your Vision*

It is hard to assess your own personality but impossible to fail to notice the personality of other people. Your pattern of thinking and acting will become your greatest tool for success. It will define the who, what and why of your eventual success. It is the sum of your physical, emotional, social and mental capacity. It is who you are and who you are perceived to be. ***Therefore...***be the visible success, think the successful abilities, embrace the social successful engagements and demonstrate the successful presence.

Attribute 9. *Take Action*

In this book, I am going to show you how to change your life forever by putting together the training and actions that will solve one of the greatest challenges that every person faces in their life, securing their income and building an income generation machine that will not let you down. This book is for people who desire more of themselves and from their peers as well as their employers. This book will open your eyes to the tactics, processes, steps and procedures to build your own passive-income machine.

Entrepreneurs struggle with their work-life balance when the game is obviously lopsided. Especially when someone else decides just how much success you are granted and how much pleasure you can have. And…you have little to say about it.

"You gain strength, courage, and confidence by every experience in which you really stop to look fear in the face. You must do the thing which you think you cannot do."

- Eleanor Roosevelt

Attribute 10. ***Intention*** / Know Your Value

Worth - Worth is that thing that tells us how much something costs or how much something can sell for. However, the price we set for ourselves is often less-than market value. Why, I'm not sure. I think that we allow it to be set by those who enjoy our company but envy our success. Therein, they reduce our worth to satisfy their egos instead of allowing us to set our worth based on our mission. Who sets your worth?

Value - Value is not only significance but also the emotion associated with worth. The older a rare artifact is the more value it attains because it demands the of worth because of its rarity also. It is the uniqueness that determines the value and... What or who is more unique than you. Who sets your value?

All of this is hugely important to me and to your goals and your future. I believe it and I believe in you. Do what's right and do it now. Your success might determine your worth but can establish your value to those around you. Which means more to you?

THAT'S WHAT THIS BOOK IS ABOUT

My Promise to You

I promise that if you follow what I teach, listen to what I say and act when I tell you to, then you will see the results of your efforts bloom into something you could never have imagined.

I promise that if you develop a plan of action and follow through with it, you will have the time and freedom that you deserve, without someone else deciding just when, just how much and just why you shouldn't get any more!

I promise that if you take notes, read every page and follow the tips, tricks, design, processes and actions that are described in this book, then you will change your life forever.

And finally, …

I promise that if you believe in yourself unconditionally and believe in me unconditionally that you will discover the instrumental strength and willingness to challenge yourself to be accountable for your success, to be responsible for your success and to be the final authority to determine your success and all the benefits that go with it.

ACKNOWLEDGMENTS

I wish to acknowledge my family. My sons, Matthew and Chris, my daughters, Traci and Kate and my wife, Kathy.

I cannot imagine life without them.

I acknowledge all the entrepreneurial pioneers whose selfless successes were a guiding light to my successes. To each who selflessly shared their "I can do" attitude and the "You can too" map for my entrepreneurial spirit.

INSIGHTS

Why Math Helps Us Understand Intuition and Perception in Internet Marketing and Online Business Development

Math helps us understand that relationships are at the core of our association with each other in time just like all things in the universe. How this relates to Internet marketing are revealed in the What, When, Why, Where and How of things. When this is taken to its maximum logical sum, the conclusion can only be that we should embrace the logical relationships between us and our customers. To better understand this theory in Internet marketing we use special tools to verify our beliefs that we have something valuable to offer, that customer desire is to learn more from us and need what we're offering, and that mathematics and testing can prove it.

Cave men used it when hunting. They learned that a single hunter might fail, be injured and starve if he hunted alone. They learned that an individual could get killed if he hunted alone. They learned that if they **added** another teammate, one or both could make a "kill" and both could eat! They learned that they could **multiply** their efforts by sending a group to hunt bigger prey and kill bigger prey and everyone could eat. They learned that of an individual was sick or hurt that they could temporarily **subtract** him from the hunt and they would still be successful hunters. They learned that they could **divide** their successful catch and share with everyone.

They learned that they could achieve success when they learned how to use...**MATH.**

The hallmark of my success was the day I considered myself a mathematician after failing every primary math lesson in grade school and high school. It clicked when I learned an unrelated lesson that it was not all about perception and intuition but about logic.

We now know that the world is not flat, and Earth is not the center of the universe though they were steadfast beliefs. Math changed that.

$E=MC^2$ may be the most well-known, definitive, exacting formula to mankind today on why the universe works the way it does. Yet.... two socks go into the washer and only one comes out, there's only one remote and you can never find it, the line you get in always becomes the longest line, you never have a penny when you need one, 100% UFO evidence seems credible and 94% have been emphatically disproved. It doesn't mean that 6% are real. The other sock is right in front of your nose. Move to another line. Get a penny...give a penny. Don't believe in UFO's.

Sometimes shit just happens and it is what it is. Go with it.

My challenge is to help you understand that your success can be guaranteed when you attack your choice of career with logic and proof. As a commercial pilot, I used training, experience, mentoring, and checklists and defined systematic approaches to EVERYTHING I did as captain. It works. I made mistakes and learned from them. Math changed that.

Science and technology has had the most profound effect on humans more in the past century than all more than a hundred centuries past. More than five-thousand years has elapsed between the two-wheeled cart and the jumbo jet. Computer power doubles about every eighteen months. The trend can only speak to inevitable change and undeniable opportunities for you right now!

When we use these well-established very powerful tools, we can help avoid failure and champion our successes when mathematics and proof are used. These are powerful tool for us to use in the 21St Century Internet marketing campaigns to address basic human problems like concerns about **Health, Sex, Money, Relationships and Freedom. 5-core niches!**

So, math is another tool to use for informed decision-making and exacting marketing. Use Simple math because it works, and you can prove it by your success. Math has become the hallmark of Internet marketing and online business success. It is now the only tool to measure your success to improve your success.

What can you learn about math can teach you about your personal success and most importantly, you can prove it too!

"We all have the strength, power,
resolve and potential to achieve any success we can imagine.
The first place to start is to imagine the success is already achieved,

Then build the effort to ensure
we get those results!

- Dr. Mark Zupo

PART 1 The Blueprint

PART 2 The Formula

PART 3 The Action Steps

Here are the 10-Commandments as a profession of your intent to be a success. Learn it and commit it to memory. Say it daily and believe in the power of the mind. Your mind.

I. This is my LIFE. I take ownership of my value and my worth, my actions and my successes.

II. I have the power to have what I want.

III. I am self-confident, and I can do anything I say I can do.

IV. Today and every day, I control my happiness, my thoughts, my actions and intention to succeed.

V. I boldly state that my mind is sharp, my heart is committed, and my course is set.

VI. There is no interference I cannot overcome.

VII. I will plan for the most and expect the best.

VIII. I'll never be the same as everyone else because I am not the same as anyone else.

IX. I can determine the journey and will control the destination.

X. I recognize my significance to others and I will gladly share my success with them."

© 2017 – As quoted by Dr. Mark Zupo

Note from the author.

This book is a collection of individual thoughts divided into 12 Modules that highlight insights to the concept and execution of starting a profitable online business.

The core steps to staring a successful online business are logical and actionable. Each Module is independent, but concepts build upon one another to define the process to construct a successful, sustainable and scalable online business.

PART 1

The Blueprint

Module 1

10 Traits of Explorers

1. **Focus**
2. **Preparedness**
3. **Conviction**
4. **Perseverance**
5. **Creativity**
6. **Curiosity**
7. **Resilience**
8. **Risk taking**
9. **Independence**
10. **A sense of higher purpose**

When you unlock your desire to succeed you also unlock your inner-explorer to champion your expedition for success and adventure.

Go for It!

The Dream

Ok, so we all know why you're here. You have the dream like so many others to make your future earning a living from the internet. It would afford you some independence, some success, some confidence, pride and of course, some more money! Read on to hear my story of how successes and failures led me to the internet.

I have always had the entrepreneurial spirit since I grew up on the farm. The defining moment for me was when I was 24 years old. I bought my first house and sold it a couple of years later and made a huge profit. …it doubled in value, so I made twice what I paid for it! I knew then that I would go on to make money in one form or another as an entrepreneur. I began investing in real estate and found my fortune in buying and renting small homes in south Florida. It wasn't long after I started that I discovered a trick to earning more with less work.

The secret was in the numbers. As you read farther down, I'll explain more about ***the number system for success*** and how it relates to Internet Marketing.

The Reality

The reality of investing in real estate was that if you made a mistake, you could lose your shirt and it could cost you a fortune, your confidence and your reputation. When you are an entrepreneur all you have is your reputation and it can be very lonely at the bottom. I learned this lesson about a year after running my real estate rental business. I owned 11 single-family homes, two Quadra-plex apartment buildings and four duplexes. Each of which earned me as little as one-hundred dollars a month to over one-thousand dollars a month…clear!

In my fourteenth month of "land-lording", I got a call from the Broward County Sherriff's department informing me that one of my homes was the center of a drug ring and would be padlocked until their investigation was complete. Yikes! It took nine-months to get it back and I lost over $50,000 dollars in lost rents, damages and fines. So much for entrepreneurship. I did recover and went on to make several hundred-thousand dollars over the next few years. What I really learned was that it took great effort over many hours, after many days of problems with tenants, water lines, toilets, roof leaks and broken windows to conclude that there had to be a better way.

The Opportunity

I picked up an Entrepreneur Magazine one day and read many great stories about opportunities that lay there waiting for me if I just sent in a dollar or two, my name and address and a coupon.

Then it happened!

I read an ad by a guy who said I could start my own business if I bought his articles on, what else, "How to Start Your Own Electronic Business"! He said that I could make thousands with little or no work. He also said that I could buy a list of interested people who would buy my articles too. I thought this was a great idea because I could market to many hundred more people with less effort than it took to manage rental properties.

...And...I was right. I placed a small display ad in the Entrepreneur magazine for the next month advertising my paper on, "How to Make Money with Your Computer". It was a five-page long, photocopied, typewritten paper report describing how to do the very

thing that made them respond to MY AD! **Genius!** It worked too. I earned over $6,000 selling two-page paper over the next four years. I mailed out over 1,200 papers to would-be entrepreneurs. Soon after, I started advertising the paper on computer "disk". It morphed from the 5" floppy to the 3-1/2" diskette before I started adding to the report. Another defining moment. One customer ordered twenty-five diskettes if he could resell them and keep some of the money.

"Are you kidding?" I said. SURE! And
my Internet business was born.

The Business

I started working from my home and my "Home Publishing Business" developed into a real electronic publishing business. With the advent of better computer programs, electronic media and other "techie stuff", I went on to sell many products and services to many thousand people across the country and across the world. One of my first foreign customers was in Africa of all places. It wasn't long though when I was getting customers complaining about missing, damaged and poor-quality materials because I wasn't paying attention to details. I also wasn't collecting names for my database. Another huge mistake.

I wasn't paying attention to customer service and quality products
because,
I was making money the easy way
and **spending it just as fast.**

The one thing that I failed to do was to run this operation like a business. When you treat it like a business, like you real job, like the only means of income that you have then it demands the respect of a real business. It demands that you devote time and resources, attention to detail, customer service, quality products and last if not least, real value.

Entrepreneurship

What it means to be an entrepreneur. After running an internet marketing business for a while I used to tell people when they asked me what I did for a living that, "I am an internet marketer." Sounds great but…those conversations didn't include what rights I had as an entrepreneur.

Right #1. I had the right to spend as much money as I had to make my business successful.

Right #2. I had the right to work tirelessly day and night, without holidays, weekends and in every spare moment that I had because I didn't have another real job at the time.

Right #3. I had the right to worry about every penny that I spent because I didn't know if I would ever see another one again!

Right #4. I had the right to give money back to unhappy customers.

Right #5. I had the right to search for new customers anywhere I could.

Right #6. I had the right to pay extra taxes, have oodles of paperwork and recordkeeping beyond my experience.

However, I was free, had independence, was my own boss and an ENTREPRENEUR!

Necessary Contributors to Successful Online Entrepreneurship

The Education

I guess that I'm not the smartest tool in the shed because it took over ten-years of trial and error to figure out simple math to simple success. I had a phone consultation with a guy named Corey Rudl, who gave me critical guidance that would prove to be invaluable over the past ten years. He was killed in a two day after our interview. It cost me nearly a thousand dollars to find out that I was dope and had wasted money for a long time. Now my new catch phrase is,

"If You Think That Education is Expensive,
Try Ignorance"
- Unknown

The Failures / Lessons

I didn't understand how using numbers to achieve my goals was critical to the measurement of my actions I took to achieve a goal. Now I understand, numbers can make you money if you use them just right. Let's see how. Let's calculate the costs of failure. What I didn't have was someone to teach me that up front.

Growing up at the DUMP

An automatic perceived failure. Go figure. Took years to get out of my own way before I could see success on my own. Emotionally expensive I guess. ***Problem – no mentor!***

Farming

One bad season…out of business! One bad season, no rain, too cold, too hot, not enough seed, varmints and poachers, 35 cents a bushel and 25 cents a bale, you figure it out. ***Problem – no mentor!***

Potato Chip Business

I ate up all the profits…and the principal. Took me pounding on doors until 10:00 at night seven-days a week to reach just a few hundred customers. Not efficient, not productive. ***Problem – no mentor!***

Aviation

Thousands for training and the industry is in the tank! When you crash one airplane into a building some say, "Gee, that's tough. When you crash three airliners into buildings…the rest is history. ***Problem – no mentor!***

Investing

Investing what you have earned in Wall Street. One example…I lost $80,000 on Enron in one day. We won't even discuss the rest. Thieves and cut-throats all. ***Problem – no mentor!***

Construction

Atlanta's boom building market through the 80" s and early 90's made me hundreds of thousands of dollars. This helped develop my interest in an Internet web-based business. Until 2007 when it all went away, so did my savings, my business, my home, cars, credit and more. ***Problem – no mentor!***

Every trial and error are an investment.
A mentor can help with better investment decisions!

The Money

Here is the important stuff, the Future!
This is what you've come here for and I won't try and disappoint you. We all have a genetic disposition to succeed. We also have a psychological disposition to let others tell us how to do it. been discovered by historical evidence in the history of man. Genetically We are wired to believe in life, death, magic, myths, misfortune and fortune. Where we place these beliefs and their order of importance is crucial to your behavioral intentions, intellectual intentions and success.

Summary:

Absolute unconditional faith in yourself and your abilities. **Get a mentor to guide you through the processes of success.**

Actions:
Build A Business Today! Develop a support system. Be genuine and sincere. Run your Internet business like a business. Educate, train, experiment and learn to earn.

"A gem cannot be polished without friction, nor a man perfected without trials."

- Seneca

Module 2

WHY IS HE RICH AND I'M NOT?

My father died when I was 10. My mother remarried, and her new husband was a business-man...of sorts. He was a farmer. He also operated a garbage dump on one corner of his expansive farm as a secondary operation to drive income. Entrepreneurial and industrious for the times but everyone was an entrepreneur before it was fashionable. Therein, he was an entrepreneur by default. In fact, everyone in the last century was entrepreneurial of sorts. They all took something they had or could do and shared it for money. I learned a great deal from the "farmer-step-father". I learned that he worked much too hard for his living. It took his personal and individual attention every hour of every day to accomplish making a living.

There is a lesson in there, right? One man can only do so much and when one man has exhausted all his energy to do that one thing...well...he is done. Limited. Held to the sum of his individual effort to earn. This I think is...NOT GOOD.

The math is simple I promise. Nothing complicated I promise. Nothing scary or limiting that you cannot do I promise. It has been established for more than 2500 years and founded in the creation of all that we know. It is also one of the best tools we have used in all recorded time.

> "Cave men used it when hunting. They learned that a single hunter might fail, be injured and starve if he hunted alone. They learned that an individual could get killed if he hunted alone. They learned that if they **added** another teammate, one or both could make a "kill" and both could eat! They learned that they could **multiply** their efforts by sending a group to hunt bigger prey and kill bigger prey and everyone could eat. They learned that of an individual was sick or hurt that they could temporarily **subtract** him from the hunt and they would still be successful hunters. They learned that they could **divide** their successful catch and share with everyone. They learned that they could achieve success when they learned how to use...**MATH.**"

We can explore the Egyptians and the pyramids, the Greeks with reasoning, the Chinese with value systems, and so on and so on from the 16th century to the 21st century math of today. There is nothing that you do that cannot be devised and calculated with mathematics. So... why not take advantage of it you ask? Because we fear it instead of embracing it. Our life's goal should be to conduct our every action using numbers, magnitude, form and relationships.

MATH IS ABOUT RELATIONSHIPS!

It never lies and never fails!

First, humans didn't invent math concepts, we discovered them. Second, math is universal. It works the same for everyone regardless of your language, culture, geography, gender or race. Math is more important in your life than you think. In fact, your very view of life depends on math. You make comparisons and averages of everything, don't you? Think about it.

From Sex to Statistics

Math is about relationships, it never lies, and it never fails. Knowing that is why we should embrace it, use it and live by its rules and ultimately succeed everywhere we want. We'll talk more about this later in the book. Look for it!

So...

WHY IS HE RICH AND I'M NOT?

Cause he / she uses math that's why!

Let's get started discovering the relationship between math and our success. We humans evaluate and analyze everything. However, we seldom do it at the right time and for the right reason. It is in our nature to question everything, but we are taught to never question and to follow orders. That's a shame because it is when we question something that we learn everything. Yet, when we ask a question we're told to, "Figure it out"! Confusing, isn't it? It is but you can see that there is math in the answer and in the question, **"figure"** it out.

Have you ever been told, "You can **count** on it?" Or maybe, "It doesn't **measure** up?"

There are many ways we use math in our everyday life. Sometimes we are aware of it and sometimes we're not. Here are a few examples.
Measuring, converting, calculating, evaluating and more.
Easy math:

I work a lot, I get paid a little,
and I don't have enough!

In the **kitchen,** we ***measure*** everything.
In the **garden,** we make *rows and count everything we plant.*
In **art,** we measure form and calculate *relationships* between them.
In **planning,** we calculate *sums and averages.*
In **banking,** we calculate *earnings and savings, ROI*
In **travel,** we plan and calculate *time, distance and costs.*
In **work,** we rely on *earnings and work for time trades.*

As you can see, we calculate, measure and evaluate EVERYTHING! So, I must ask you, "Then why don't we use them to make our life easier instead of complaining that we don't have enough time, energy, effort, resources or tools?"
That's what I am going to try and teach you here today.

The Math of Success

I'm going to teach you to LOVE math one number at a time. I will teach you very complex formulas and make them easy to use, like;

Probability, What Happens When You Do That...

Likelihood, What Happens If You Do That?

Possibility, What Could Happen If You Don't Do That?

Confidence - What You Can Make Happen.

Proof - What the World Wants to See.

Pi - Simple Formulas
(Not rhubarb, apple or cherry)

ROI - What You Get for What You Give

Leverage - How to Use What You Have Now

Investment - What You Will Promise to Deliver

Possibility - What Happens When?

Theory - What Happens If?

Force - How to Make It Happen!

Measurement - How to Measure Your Success

Testing – How to Test Your Processes

Dimensions - What Is the Big Picture

Guarantee - What Your Promise Means in the End

You see, it's not as frightening as you thought, is it? Right! Well, just wait because it is going to get a whole lot more exciting when you see just what is possible. Without mathematics, you ignore and forfeit your opportunities to achieve great things. Sit up, pay attention. Your success depends on it.

Let's get started.

I have a few questions for you. "How much do you want to earn in a year?" Don't be afraid, just blurt it out. $100,000? A million Dollars? More? Less? Somewhere in between? It really doesn't matter but you must quantify it to measure your success, right?

I'm going to show you how **order relates to *automatic income systems! Can* I get an**
"Oh Yeah!".

I'm going to show you how **effort** (energy) ***one-time delivers results many times!*** **Can I get a, "Wahoo!"**

I'm going to show you why...wait for it...wait for it...

There is a ***probability*** that if you produce a product ***one time*** that there is a ***likelihood*** that it can be reproduced ***many times*** and there is a real ***possibility*** that if marketed *correctly* and *consistently* that you can have ***confidence*** you'll see the ***proof*** of your *labor and effort* at the **BANK!**
There we go, <u>you're first math model lesson in success.</u>

"What gets measured gets managed"
- Unknown

You Must Quantify Your Success to Measure Your Success

Math can help you save money, make money, manage time and evaluate, regulate and control effort to achieve maximum results!

SO, how do you like math so far?

ADDITION -

Here's where addition started with my father on the farm.
In his era, the formula looked something like this:

Effort + Action = Results

When he worked the farm, his actions were many and his results were few. Well-deserved and well-earned but...few. He worked, worked, worked and got paid. (Sometimes). Well, in my book, that sucks! A better formula would look something like this:

Big Effort / Small Effort One Time + Fast and Decisive Well-Calculated Action One Time = Huge Recurring Passive Results FOREVER!

OK, so a bit overboard and a mouthful but you see the difference. I have come to understand that the better way to create wealth is to make your business a multiplying endeavor that doesn't require your presence. The key was to find such a business that didn't require me to work, work, and work just to get paid once. The better business was one that required small effort upfront that could be duplicated and then deliver results forever!

My doctor can only see me and so many other patients in a day, a week or a year, right? A plumber, a hairdresser, painter, landscaper, or computer geek can only serve or service a limited number of people in the same time as well. Again, right?

WHY WOULD YOU LIMIT YOUR EXPOSURE THE SAME WAY?

Multiplication -

So here is where multiplication comes in. It is about exposure. You see, it is simple, right? Nothing complicated about math after a little understanding and comprehension of how it works for you...or how it can work for you. How you can multiply your effort to maximize your results.

You do something once, sell it many times and collect income virtually and possibly ***FOREVER!***

This is the concept of a "royalty" on your efforts.

I LOVE multiplication! I live for multiplication! This concept is hugely attractive and the foundation for everything that I do in business today. I applaud people for their ability to produce fantastic individual works of art or products of value from their individual effort...BUT I SHOUT the virtues of someone who earns from a single effort repeatedly. Multiplying their single effort repeatedly.

Division - There is good and bad division. We will focus on the good division. You can divide the workload. You can share the profits that you would never have made when you divide your effort among affiliates.

Equality (Balance) - The balance of success is seen in science, opportunity and achievement. Someone once said that the best evidence of your success and achievement is realized at the bank. I believe it and have proved it many times.

Subtraction - You can first subtract the money that you will not lose by following those that have succeeded before you are having tried and experimented with their money and effort. You will subtract your costs from your expenses and the balance shall be greater to your advantage if you follow a prescribed program or protocol. **(Hint - Get a Mentor).**

Average - Your average success is determined by your average expense, effort and intentions.

Conversion - You might get a million people to click on your website and half a million to click through to your offer and a quarter million to opt in to your offer and 100,000 to click on the offer sales page BUT....if you don't convert the first visitor...a sale will never happen and they will just be tire-kickers. P.S. No money made.... Ugghhhhh.

I believe that everyone secretly wants to be wealthy to enjoy the finer things in life and can contribute to other people's needs and wants too.

The problem is that many people associate getting rich or wealthy with either a single opportunity like winning the lottery or an inheritance or a lifetime of hard work, failure, struggle and more failure!

That's sad.

Why it is necessary to struggle your entire life for a small piece of the pie is a predicament? The very thought of it stops people, like a freight train grinding to a halt, from ever trying to do anything and realizing their dreams. If someone does try once and fails...well...eventually they will quit trying and settle for a life of mediocrity and servitude. Not going to happen to you..is it?

BUT…that is never going to happen to you, right?

"Trying and failing is better than
not trying and wailing"
-Dr. Mark Zupo

Entrepreneurial failure is just as predictable as entrepreneurial success.

There are symptoms and signs of each. The systems of a life without a plan are so visible that we choose to ignore it rather than attempt to change it likely because we fear change, failure and disappointment. Perceptions include:

- Work pressure to perform
- Demanding bosses who are heartless
- Fear of losing one's job
- Routine that drain our energy
- Competition from peers

- Failure to build an "income-business"
- Lack of self confidence
- Income depravation

--- There is a better way!

Since 2012, there has been an explosion in the eLearning opportunities. Finally, Colleges and universities have embraced online teaching and learning and a HUGE market for: Self-Paced learning.

<u>Self-paced learning has grown from nothing to more-than a $60.5-Billion!</u>

What's the math behind this new form of success? **It is the appeal to the masses that make it attractive. The convenience, autonomy and control.**

The eLearning market is expected to grow steadily at nearly 7.6% a year.

<u>That's more-than $4-Billion more every year!</u>

What does that mean for you? I'll tell you.

Whether you try your hand at it and fail or you try your hand at it and succeed, either way you have the unbelievable opportunity to cash in just from your own little corner of your world.

DO THE MATH!

This is where I tell you how to, "Start Your Personal Success Revolution." and how you are going to do it through - **Multiple Streams Mastery™.**

I'm going to do it in a way that you are absolutely going to LOVE IT! ...and hopefully use it to find your success, independence and achievements.

Geometry	- The shapes
Astronomy	- The stars
Physics	- The energy & force
Calculus	- The change

If the probability of entrepreneurial business success is only 4%, how many time must one try before they are guaranteed success? An entrepreneur knows however, that there is no guarantee of success...or is there?

The laws of nature are steady and trustworthy. Knowing that then one can rely on them to be true, right?

If an entrepreneur tries to succeed and fails 96% of the time, that leaves a 4% opportunity the second time, right?

Thinking ahead, how many time can an entrepreneur try until their success is a given?

Each time the opportunity is smaller but so is the probability of success until there is no option but to succeed!

With training, experience, mentoring and determination, success can be guaranteed. The laws of math do not lie.

"The life of a mathematician is dominated by an insatiable curiosity, a desire bordering on passion to solve the problems he is studying."
-- Jean Dieudonne

Summary:
Systems, Processes, Automation and Action

Action:

Quantify your value to access your wants, needs and desires

Move your "zeros" to the left.

Before - $.00 / After - $000,000.00

"Decimals have a point."
- Unknown

Module 3

Wealthy or Rich Formulas

My Personal Formula for Success:
"Find out what people want and give it to them before they need it"
-Dr. Mark Zupo

Make no mistake about it, my step-father wasn't close to what I would consider rich or wealthy, but he was well-off enough to deliver a healthy, plentiful and good life to us. He worked hard for it and so did we. When I asked you previously, "how much money do you want to earn this or next year?", it wasn't because I wanted you to guess. It was because I wanted you to know how much you could and would earn. I wanted to see if you would calculate it if you could calculate it. If you had it in stone and knew what it was going to take to get to your goal. Even if you had a goal. You see, I wanted to know that you had done the "math". If you had clarity using 2500-year-old principles of math.

It is a ridiculously easy question to answer...if you've done the math. If you haven't then how do you expect to achieve the result you expect?

When I asked myself the question, "How I would make a million dollars?", the answer is simple. I did the math. It would take about 30 years making about $100,000 per year. Wait! You say. That doesn't add up. Well, yes it does. Once you factor all the variables in it does add up...and it stinks. *Note - the costs and averages stated below are determined by the U.S. Bureau of Labor Statistics averages for the standard four-member family living in the U.S. Add more people, add more costs.

$100,000 per year: minus taxes @ 34%.

$100,000 minus 34,000 = $66,000

$66,000 minus living expenses, food, clothing, shelter = $41,000

$41,000 minus medical, school, children, travel, fun = $12, 000

$12, 000 minus losses, repairs, maintenance, etc. = $8,400

$8,400 per year savings X 30 years (interest considered) =

Wait for it...

Wait for it...

...wait even longer for it...

...a whopping **$252,000! In the bank.**
AFTER 30 YEARS!

First, who the "H. E. - double-LL"
can save $8,400 a year?

Who can save anything on a $50,000 a year salary. Remember, that was assuming that you made $100,000 a year! Now factor that your measly J.O.B didn't even pay you that much! Odds are that likely it didn't, doesn't and will never pay that much, right?

WHAT! Where's my MILLION DOLLARS?

So, let's explore odds.

ODDS -

In this book, odds are closely associated with **percentages** and **rates**. When trying to accomplish a goal it is imperative that we consider what the percentages of success are, and the rate of success based on some predefined numbers. One can set their sights on a goal and work for as long and as hard as it takes to achieve that goal and the number of failures they experience along the way. Here we need to explore whether we want to be rich or we want to be wealthy. There is a difference and a critical one at that.

The law of large numbers – a million-to-one odds happen more than 300 times a day. Not so daunting, now is it?

Often, we see others continue to try to achieve their financial and entrepreneurial goals for as long as it takes until they throw their hands up in defeat and accept failure no matter how long it took to fail! Notice I said, "Fail". You see, continuing to try and ignore the math that would all but guarantee success is...well...stupid.

If you had to fill in this math equation, what would you put?
___________ + ___________ = Big Bucks

If you're into personal development, you might put:
"Knowledge + Skills = Big Bucks"

And if you're into online marketing then maybe you'd put: "Traffic + Conversion = Big Bucks"

Well, I'd like to share something with you...

Making a living online is simple. (Not necessarily easy, but surely, it's simple.) It simply requires these two ingredients:

Ingredient 1 is: Opportunity.
Ingredient 2 is: Action.

So, my formula is:

"Opportunity + Action = Results (Big Bucks)"

Having the <u>intellect</u> to see opportunity, and the <u>guts</u> to act are key factors. If you just see opportunity, and don't act, then you'll end up frustrated and always talking about what could've been.

If you just act, without good opportunities, then you'll end up working way too HARD and never working SMART.

No one can guarantee your success. My success is not typical, and my results are not typical because I am not typical. Just like you. Your success will be determined by you and only you.

"I would rather *earn 1% off 100 people's efforts* than 100% *of my own efforts."*

- John D. Rockefeller

In 1897, the Italian Economist, Vilfredo Pareto, studied patterns of money and wealth. He found that 80% of the wealth was controlled by just 20% of the people. He also understood another interesting thing, there were uneven relationships in other areas of people's lives.

People seemed to ignore that their effort singularly could only produce so much income. The people who recognized that duplicating their effort through other people would gain higher rewards of income. Basically, one man can only do so much, but many men can do more.

DO THE MATH!

Multiply your efforts to reach the masses and you must gain more than you ever could appealing to just one at a time.

Which person do you think is the most successful?

The one with the most money?

The one with the most friends?

The one with the cure for all diseases?

The one who looks back on their life without regrets?

DO THE MATH!

Which would you rather have, a penny doubled every day for a month or a million dollars?
Hint...

Take the penny compounded every day for the month. It adds up to over $5 Million dollars. I just saved you a $4-Million-dollar loss. *You're welcome.*
So now that you are a millionaire, let's talk about how much you are worth and how much you agree to sell your time for.

"MATH - Not just another four-letter word!"
- Dr. Mark Zupo

When I started Internet marketing back in early 2001, my goal was to earn $5 from every customer I could get to pay me for a $5 report that I mailed to them. It cost me a stamp and an envelope.

My average was about three-a-day. Let's do the math.
$15-a-day equates to $75-a-week. (Pretty much sucks, right?). I had to change what I was doing to increase that yield.

I decided to plan.

I wanted to earn $100,000 a year from my enterprise. I wanted it so badly that I would have done anything to make it happen. I was working for the government in a lifeless, soul-crushing, energy-stealing, dream crushing job for a demanding, overbearing ogre of a boss.

With a plan, I increased my profits 10-fold in just seven months. Still not up to the steady amount or the $100,000 goal I set for myself. It would take another two years before I got there. It wasn't until 2005 until I made my first sale from another guy who gave my name to another girl who bought my report. WOW, an affiliate before I knew what an affiliate was!

It didn't take long for me to set up an automatic sales program and start to earn the income I expected. I went from earning $15-a-day to more than $500 a day! And the earnings have continued steadily since.

How would an extra $500 a day help you? How would an extra $1,000 a week help you? How about an extra $5,000 a month?

What I learned was to reverse-engineer my earnings from the back forward from what I wanted to earn to and calculate what I had to do to earn that money.

If you want to earn an extra $1,000 a month...then you set a goal to make $33 a day.

If you want an extra $5,000 a month...then you set a goal to make $161 a day.

Do this for thirty-days and presto! You're there.
Then...**RINSE AND REPEAT!**

DO THE MATH!

$100,000 a year is just $273 a day!
So, how many people would you have to touch to earn the $273 a day.

---100, 1,000, 10,000?

I'll show you how.

There are no guarantees and the results are based on your experience, effort, energy, income, support and more BUT it reveals the possibilities, right?
When $15 a day becomes enough then $15 an hour will also become enough. When that doesn't become enough then $30,000 a year will never be enough.

Anyone can do that.

Eventually, $100,000 will never become enough because you will have gained enough knowledge to work your plan and make even more, right?

3% of your success happens
just because you let it happen.
97% of your success happens
because you made it happen!

- Dr. Mark Zupo

Summary:

Do the Math,
Help Other People,
Be Genuine,
Reach the masses.

Action:

Act and calculate your own success. Reverse engineer your wants to break down the actions and the goals. Minimize your effort by minimizing the work into small chunks.

Module 4

7 Important Lessons I learned From My Failures

"There are only two times I feel stress... Day and Night"

- Unknown

Shortly after hurricane Andrew took out south Florida in 1992, I found myself wondering what I would do if I was still living in south Florida. I was struggling to make a decent living working for the government.

There was no social media to speak of. No Facebook, no Twitter, no YouTube...no nothing. Just the Internet in its infancy.

As I was exploring the "new" Internet I discovered that in the "income" magazines that some other people were using it to advertise products and services. I saw dollar signs and dug in. My intention was to escape from the clutches of the federal "job" and make money on my own.

Fast forward to April 2011, I officially finished my first book and registered my business name as a corporation. I was in business! Yahoo. Pretty good for a 40-year old guy who didn't even own a computer! Sad that it took me 19 years! Ugghhhhh.

My goal was to make a decent living using the Internet and not have to report to a boss ever again. EVER AGAIN!

It was a goal achieved.

I would have never imagined what would follow that glorious day. I started to make more money than most people would ever see in a week, a month or a year for that matter. My first lesson was when I took on a partner. Let's say that after a few months of partnership, it ended abruptly. The key word is "part." I shared most of my profits when he did only a small part of the work.

Bad idea. He then ran off with my money and my secretary!

"The best lesson earned are
the hardest lessons learned"

- Dr. Mark Zupo

I got burned badly, financially. An eye-opening lesson. My hope is that by sharing this story you will avoid the same mistakes as you search for your independence.

Your desire to reach your dreams should prevent you from settling on mediocrity.

What I've gained is a huge dose of wisdom in the process of my failure experiences. The following are 7 of the most important of all the lessons.

1. I Have Gained Tremendous Wisdom in the Process of Failing. I Accept Responsibility for My Actions and Inactions

Ignoring one's problems is simply wrong. Failure to realize that inaction is as wrong as the incorrect action can be devastating. It's somewhat naive. Your naivete can lead to unsound decisions that ultimately cost me a fortune. *Tip – Get a mentor.*

I failed to measure my success and the specific marketing strategies, demographics and general business habits of my best buyers.

When it boils down to fault, it was mine and my inaction was costly. Therein...no excuses. I owned it.

2. Embrace the Rules for Goal-setting

As important as EVERYONE has EVER said, goals are of supreme importance. Why we people fail to believe it is beyond me, but I am as guilty as anyone else. But...not anymore.

However, will I (or you) ever attain anything if (we) never have a goal to strive for? Today I live by the calendar and set hourly, daily, weekly and yearly goals.

Clarity is the key and action is the engine that drives goal-driven success.

How much money do you want to make?
How much do you want to make this year? This month? This week?
How will you do it?
What plan will you follow?
What action will you take to make it happen?

What action will you take if it fails to happen?

More importantly...What will you do to get to that goal?

...and so, on and so on.

My primary goal was to replace my current income. I was making just under $5,000 a month. I was also struggling to keep my family fed, clothed and housed.

My goal was to make $10,000 a month for 3-months in a row. I achieved that goal even though it took me about 5 months to do so.

Do you think it would ever have happened if I didn't have a hard and fast definitive goal? I don't think so. P.S. I resigned six months to the day that I almost doubled my salary.

Can I get a Yeehaaw here?

3. Develop a Support System

Once you become an entrepreneur, pride can be your worst enemy. It becomes your next barrier to a success-driven mindset. You begin to think that you don't need anyone else and can do it all alone.

As you become independent. You become defensive to criticism, even from those with more experience. It will become necessary to fall back on an independent system of support people who are impartial to your dreams and aspirations.

Sometimes you must let your ego take a back seat and listen to someone else make creative criticism...on your behalf.

It's for your own good. *Tip* – **Get a devoted, experienced, dedicated and engaged mentor. (Someone like me!).**

A mentor is powerful if used correctly. A mentor will direct your mastermind, a self-imposed group of like-minded supporters and confidants with your best interest in mind. People who keep you accountable and provide backing when you need it most.

I was resistant to support, outside influence but it was most resistant to outside influence. In fact, I that is when I needed it most.

This past year was revealing. It let me better understand just how important a mastermind group is and it was proven when my business really started to flourish because of it.

4. Understand That It Is a Business

As I stated just a moment ago, it is business. My business. What I needed to learn and well understand that as a business, it required the respect of a true business and should not include emotion as a guide to accepting help.

Now, when we talk about the Internet, The Internet becomes even more important because of the intangible nature of online business. In the past, businesses were and still are brick and mortar representations of someone's labor and enterprise. Today it is very different. Businesses are represented online and can be perceived as intangible.

As with brick-and-mortar business, all required systems and support are the same. Taxes, insurance, customer service, materials, supplies and service.

So why not accept online business as an Internet-based business the same as a traditional brick-and-mortar business. The typical one-man one-stop-shop is frequently how Internet businesses run because of the digital tools available today.

Now I have developed trust and delegation as key attributes. It has paid off too.

Now I use my resources, tools and assets to my advantage. I work less and get paid more. That's the best formula ever!

5. Share and Share Alike

Someone once said that, "The hole you give through is the same hole that you get through". I think that it means a form of reciprocity. A statute of business ethics and generosity.

I am always rewarded but I don't act to reap the reward I act to provide benefit to others. It is the law of reciprocity. What you give always comes back to you.

The lesson is to provide value, significance and quality. Value rules.

6. F.O.C.U.S.

Follow / One's / Course / Until / Successful

No better statement was ever made. One system, one action, one model, one plan, one goal and one intent. Learning everything to be great will override anything to just be good.

Adjust your goals to achievable exercises. If it isn't achievable in the time allotted, then it isn't the right focus of your energy. Taking the first step is more important than building an empire overnight.

"Every road starts with the first brick"

- Dr. Mark Zupo

7. NEVER, NEVER, NEVER Quit!

Don't ever stop trying or experimenting. The biggest failures in history were also the same people who are known for their success. Be persistent, never accept no for an answer and endure failure to be treated as a learning experience or opportunity.

It's not easy to fail because it eats at your very being.

Persistence is one of the fundamental traits of an explorer!
Practice, Practice, Practice!

Your results are the most valuable of lessons whether they are good or bad! Either way you learn the best way to succeed.

My journey is just that...mine. Yours is as important to you. Well defined, specific and personal. No one else can claim it but you.

I can only hope that you've learned something from this that will help you on your journey too.

Be brave, be safe and be generous.

PART 2

The Formula

Module 5

Guaranteed Opportunity

"It's hard to wait around for something you know might never happen; but it's harder to give up when you know it's everything you want."

- Unknown

There are five core problems that plague people today. They are:
Health
Money
Sex
Relationships
And freedom. (Or the lack of)

These aren't in any specific order of importance however each has a part in the other. Jokingly, if you have problems with sex then you have problems with all the others...Lol.

However, the foundation remains the same. Find a way to help people do, avoid, understand, engage or overcome the basic problem in their life and you become the expert that they will look for to help. That my friends are now your life's goal if you want to be an Internet entrepreneur and online business owner. A worthy cause for humanity.

Help people:

- ✓ **Make money**
- ✓ **Save money**
- ✓ **Make time**
- ✓ **Save time**
- ✓ **Avoid pain**
- ✓ **Increase pleasure**

Do one or more of those things and you will have found the secret formula for success. When you find the way to monetize your "product or service" then the profit will follow.

First things first. Guaranteed opportunity does not mean guaranteed success. Historical examples of determination and endurance are seen throughout history. Some more famous than others and some less well known but none-the-less important to us right now. Abraham Lincoln is one such story. His failures are less well known than his successes as the 16th President ending slavery. His failures are so numerous that one would wonder why he ever tried once having failed so frequently.

Let's examine his failures considering his successes. We'll discuss why these are hugely important to us today and how we can use them to avoid the same pitfalls in our endeavor to become free of debt and the burden of "owing our soul to the company store".

Abraham Lincoln's track record:

- 1832—Ran for state legislature and ***lost***.
- 1832—***Lost his job***.
- 1836—Tried to become speaker of the state legislature (after his election in 1834), ***and lost***.
- 1840—Sought to become elector and ***lost***.
- 1843—Ran for congress and ***lost***.
- 1848—Ran for re-election for congress (after being elected in 1846) and ***lost***.
- 1849—Sought job of land officer in home state, ***was rejected***.
- 1854—Ran for U.S. senate, ***and lost***.
- 1856—Sough Vice-Presidential nomination, ***was rejected***.
- 1858—Ran for U.S. senate, ***and lost*—again**!

As you can see he was successful at losing and failing. Oh yes, the times were different as they are today, I know but they still represent a wealth of knowledge and experience that we need to capitalize on.

OK, let's do some math.

He failed at least 33% of the time.

BUT...

That also meant that he succeeded at least 50% of the time. The important numbers and statistics are that when he won or succeeded **it was in GRAND style!** ...and it was the winning we remember most.

Babe Ruth was another splendid example of losing and winning. Who was he and why is he important to us today?

Name: George Herman Ruth, Jr. (Babe)
Born: Baltimore, Maryland, 1895–1948

Babe Ruth is the single greatest presence in the history of American baseball, recognized as "the slugger." Ruth and his teammates won seven pennants and four World Series. Ruth hit more than 40 homers per season in 11 seasons—a record never equaled—and 60 in one season. Before he retired in 1935, Ruth hit 714 career home runs, a record few players have even approached. Babe Ruth was a tremendous failure at the same time as he was a tremendous success. Ruth struck out 1,330 times in his career. His lifetime batting average was .342 which meant he didn't hit the ball 66% of the time he came up to bat! Please explain to me how someone who misses the mark 66% of the time become the success-legend that Babe Ruth is today? Well, when we break it down, do the math we can easily see how.

Ruth's failures:

- Struck out 1,330 times in his career.
- His lifetime batting average of .342
- He didn't hit the ball nearly 67% of the time he came up to bat. But when he did......Oh My!

Ruth's Successes:

- World Series Champion, 1916, 1918, 1926, 1928
- 714 career home runs and record 40 home runs in each of 11 seasons
- Led League in home runs 12 times
- Highest all-time slugging pct. (.690)
- 7-time American League Pennant winner
- The Associated Press' Athlete of the Century, 1999
- The Sporting News' Greatest Player of All Time, 1999

To the point, failure is the brainchild of success. It supports experience and effort in the battle for supremacy. BUT, without one there is no other! Why is this important? Let's see why. Without the experience of failure, one would never be able to find the solution, the answer, the explanation, the resolution, the result or the clarification we need to move forward. That coupled with determination and resolve can be the transition from failure to success.

THEN, when we learn from it we publicize and share it with others. That is why it is important. To learn from other's mistakes a failure to avoid some of them when we seek success. We will still fail but maybe in a less-grand manner. That's where I come in. The traps for most of us are:

- Selling our time for money.
- Selling our dreams to a demanding boss or job
- Living someone else's dream
- Struggling to get ahead of the game

These are traps almost impossible to escape from, without help! Without a mentor, a guide, who has the experience and more. You will fall out of love with your life's passions when someone else tells you how to run it. Travel for work takes the fun out of one of life's pleasures and benefits, travel for the thrill of exploration. Your job becomes the root of your unhappiness and discomfort. You become married to your J.O.B... and begin to hate it. Shame, because that isn't how the dream goes. At least your dream, right?

Let's talk about "guaranteed opportunity" before we get depressed about your life. So, let's talk about a plan. An actionable plan. A formula for "success." A YES plan. We'll start by looking at the breakdown. I love to break things down to their smallest. I can relate to that and hope that you can too.

When you must endure something unpleasant I always say that, "I can endure anything for a few minutes or an hour but longer might take more effort." Small steps to get to the big steps. So, I've found that a three-step process works for business. Here's a three-step process that you can try for your business:

1. Reverse engineer your needs from the back forward. Figure out how much you need or want and then to go backwards to see how you will attain that goal.

2. Break down the price that you will sell a product for, figure what you want to earn a month and calculate how many people / sales it will take to achieve that amount!

Easy as pie!

Then... scale up your service by increasing the amounts and presto!

Imagine you get the attention of 1,000 people, 10,000 people, 100,000 people, how many people would it take to make 100 sales, 1,000 sales, 100,000 sales? Then...

DO THE MATH!

There's a twist to this formula too to earn even more from less. I'll bet you can get behind that one, right? I'll share that in a few.

We'll talk larger packages to smaller audiences.

We'll talk smaller incremental payments from many more people.

We'll talk recurring payments from more people.

Read on...

Another Formula for Success

Target Income = Sales X Price

Example: $20,000 a month = $5,000 product X 4 sale a month.

That didn't hurt a bit, did it?

Don't be the person who misses out on opportunities when they present in your life because you took too long to see it, recognize it and act on it. Be the kind of person other people marvel at because you attract money, you attract success and attract the opportunities that others pass up and regret not acting on.

Consider this...

A. There will be over 3-BILLION Internet users by the end of 2018!

B. The Internet users has grown by over 600% and is holding that growth rate now for some time.

C. It is expected that these will be over 5-Billion users by the end of 2020!

D. Internet usage that are indicated by user preferences:

•Health	-	62.2%
•Research	-	62%
•Shopping	-	58%
•Banking	-	50.1%
•Employment	-	45.5
•Travel Reservations		43%
•Social Interactions		15.2%

E. <u>The FASEST growing segment - Social Interaction!</u>

F. The second FASTEST growing segment is <u>MOBILE!</u>

<u>Summary:</u>

Using the application of incremental instances of energy and effort to achieve your goals. Failure can lead to success. Reverse engineer your goals.

<u>Action:</u>

Build MASSIVE / PASSIVE / INCOME. Target your needs, wants and desires. Establish your formula.

Module 6

My Failure Resume

I always thought I would be a millionaire,
didn't you?

- Mark Zupo

If I have never learned anything it is that I must think like an owner. No effort is ever complete unless its eventual failure or success is owned. You must own it and you must believe it.

Here are some ways for you to understand the relationship to your beliefs and how understanding how numbers, simple math can help you make more money, save time and increase generosity through Internet marketing.

1. The Numbers Game
2. Belief in The Numbers
3. How List-Building Numbers Are Crucial
4. Building-Block Number-ology Tools
5. How Numbers Can Conquer Fear and Failure

Fear and failure are
the world's best employees.

They show up every day.
They Work very hard 24/7.
They expect to be paid.

They belong to the peer support union
They have only one job...To see that you fail.

Numbers (Math) can **fire** fear and failure!

Chance are, you had the same dream too. So why does the other guy, who is no smarter than you, has no more desire than you and no more opportunity than you, make a million dollars and you don't?

So why are they rich and you're not? It's simple...training! The very training that I provide my students across the world. Check it out.

CLICK HERE - Multiple Streams Mastery.

If you don't have a rich uncle...
If you didn't win the lottery...
If you didn't win a Nobel prize...

Likely you haven't become an overnight success either.

There's really no such thing. It takes work, dedication, focus and... TRAINING! More importantly, it's a journey and you need to know the right path to take.

Find out which way to turn when you get to the fork
in the "road-to-success". Check it out here...

Your Success Now!

P.S. Take a minute to hear what I must say about real success. I made my first million before I was 40 and it took me 30 years…without help.
This is all about how you can avoid the time-wasting mistakes I made that cost me 29 extra years to find my success! This is about

choice.

The first step is to develop a way to "funnel" money to you. Better yet, you "funnel" customers to you that you can sell to repeatedly. Let's see how we can do this.

PART - A

When we are done with this exercise you should have a clearer understanding of how I use math to build an online business and how I use math to sustain it as well.

Let's say that I want to earn $100,000 in a year. That's twelve months. We're going to average and round for ease of understanding so don't get too critical here.

There are 52 weeks a year. To earn $100,000 a year you would have to earn about $2,000 a week (rounding remember?). So, take two weeks off.

$2,000 X 52 weeks equals $100,000!

Now I had to figure out how to earn $2,000 a week, right?

So, I put together a 12-step training and membership program that sold for $400 up front then it was $97 a month after that for continued training and access to my Facebook private membership community.

Here's where the math makes me excited!

Here we go. I need $2,000 a week, right? That means that I can sell 5 training programs a week and that will give me the $2,000 a week that I want.

OR

I can sell 4 training programs a week and 4 - $97 memberships.

OR

I can sell 3 training programs and 4 - $97 memberships....and so on and so on. You get the idea, right?

PART - B

Now that you have boiled down what you need, now we can figure out how many people it will take to accomplish our goal of $2,000 a week.

This is the fun part. The global Internet community totals about a BILLION people. How hard do you think it will be to get about 100 people to check my product, service or training out? Let's see what 100 customers can do for me.

Keep this in mind... There are about 3-billion people around the world who have Internet, which is about 45 percent of the global population. Approximately 2.1 billion people have social media accounts, and approximately 1.7 billion people have active social media accounts.

If I got the attention of 100 people a week to opt in to your $400 training services or your $97 a month membership, that would give me the opportunity to sell to as many of them as you can. Let's say that only 10% buy into my training or membership.

That's ten people a week who pay me $400 for training. 10 X $400 equals $4,000 A WEEK! Keep going - $4,000-week X 50 weeks equals $200,000! A year.

What if I suck at sales? Let's boil it down even more. Imagine that only 5 people buy my training?

5 X $400 equals $2,000 a week. $2,000-week X 50 weeks equals - $100,000 a year.

What if only 5 people opt in to my membership? That's 5 people a week X $97 a month which equals $1,940 X 50 weeks a year? Drum-roll please.... $97,000 a year!

What If? I had more than one product or service?

What If? I had more than one membership site?

What If? I continually advertised for new customers?

What If? I had several digital, electronic, virtual, passive products at $97?

What IF?

I hope by now that you can see how the smallest math calculations can mean big business for you and me. Simple math equals simple results. It doesn't have to be more complicated than that. Once broken down, it becomes an achievable goal, right?

Hopefully from this little exercise you can see how someone can make it happen when it is in its simplest form. Now you can see it, so you can do it, right?

The Magic of 100

As you've probably guess by now, I love the number 7 and the number 100. Let me show you how both of those came to be my favorites. There is something that I learned from a friend in the past number of years. It is the benefits of a "Micro-membership" site.

I never expected to see the results that I did until I started my own "Micro-membership" site(s). Notice that it is multiple(s). Yes, I have several.

So, what is a Micro-membership site?

It can be a huge and simple platform for you to teach other people with your own knowledge, experience, expertise, passions and skills. It can be profitable, somewhat passive, recurring and engaging.

Here are some of the benefits of a Micro-membership site:

- You get paid repeatedly
- You can start with very little content
- It only requires a little maintenance
- There are very few support issues
- It can be in your preferred niche
- It usually has a long retention rate

What is possible to make from your Micro-membership site?

Let's just look at members at only $10 a month:

- 10 members @ $10 per month = $100
- 50 members @ $10 per month = $500
- 100 members @ $10 per month = $1,000
- 500 members @ $10 per month = $5,000
- 1,000 members ______________________

@ $10 per month = $10,000 every month!

Now imagine bigger numbers!

100 people?

1,000 people?

how about 10,000 people?

How about increasing the monthly fee?

$29? / $49? / $79?

$100 a month?

Now up your price for personal training to $5,000, $10,000 or even $50,000 a client! It is being done every day and can be done every day. If I can imagine it then I can do it!

Do some more math to get even more excited.

Imagine 50 people paying you for specialized, personal

mentoring or training.

10 people X $2,500 equals $25,000
25 people X $5,000 equals $125,000!
50 people X $10,000 equals $500,000!

100 people X $25,000 equals $2,500,000!

BETTER YET - imagine that you charge $5,000 or $10,000 or $25,000 for a single training seminar that lasts for only 3-days or 5-days or 7-days!

In an exotic location!

Imagine that only 50 people come.

That's 50 X $5,000 = $250,000 in a weekend!
That's 50 X $10,000 = $500,000 in a weekend!
That's 50 X $25,000 = $1,250,000 in a weekend!

Again, it is done every day, every week and every week. Even from people that suck at sales. Even from people that suck at training. Even from people that barely know what they're doing.

Play with the numbers, divide, multiply and add it all up. Do this even if you suck at everything! It can work. It does work. How hard do you think it would be to find 100 people out of a billion to play along?

Do it. DO IT!

AND THEN...DO IT AGAIN

...and again...**and again!**

"Money is multiplied in practical value depending on the number of W's you control in your life: what you do, when you do it, where you do it, and with whom you do it."

—Timothy Ferriss

I've always been straight forward with people when it comes to acting. I don't accept excuses. Ever. A lot of my formal training was as a commercial pilot. I refer to aviation a great deal because it fits almost every situation well.

In aviation, there are a few rules. They are steadfast and finite. When we sway from them people get hurt and equipment get damaged. There is a checklist for EVERYTHING! Follow the checklist and everything goes smoothly. Sway from the checklist and... well, you know.

In aviation, there are four real rules that govern everything. They are:

Planning eliminates the opportunity for most problems before they happen.

Problems that come up require a solution
...immediately.

Decisions are required to find solutions
...immediately.

Actions result in decision-making that solves problems...immediately.

As a highly-trained individual, I always follow those rules as a part of everything I do. And guess what, so do you even if you don't think so. To a degree anyway.

Almost all the world's highest-trained professionals are also the most successful in their field. They train, train, plan, train, practice and train some more. They all start learning about their passion when young and are willing to absorb everything about it. You can bet that the most highly-trained people know their strengths and weaknesses and do what it takes to use them or defeat them.

When creativity, passion, belief and action come together, nothing can stop someone from being successful, whatever success means to them.

The MATH Behind My Success...

90 % Perseverance + 10% Inspiration

What's behind your success? I imagine that it is about the same formula. Feel comfortable that you and I are always working to achieve our goals. Always. How much effort we put into it may differ as will our individual success differ. There are no promises and no guarantees. There are processes, procedures and formulas to help guide us to make it happen and do it in a safe and achievable way.

I remember high school all too well. I hated it. I remember thinking that I was in prison and wanted to escape. I thought that I was smarter than my teachers. (What kid doesn't? Lol). The problem was that I was not a math whiz. In fact, I flunked Algebra three times and it was almost what kept me from graduating in my 12th year. That meant summer school! Ugghhhhh. More prison longer during the hottest time of the year! P.S. My school didn't have Air Conditioning.

I sat in the classroom for two full summers, (8-weeks) to pass Algebra 1. I stared out the window the entire time. It sucked. I was a prisoner. Who needed this crap anyway? What good will it ever do for me? I couldn't care less. When my "sentence" was over I finally passed Algebra 1 with a D. It satisfied the administration and I eventually graduated. Straight B's and a D. Who cares right?

I have a PhD. now!

OK, so. What does it mean to me today. A lot. In fact, it means everything. To say the least, I've become a math whiz now. Easily calculating EVERYTHING in my life. Time, distance, earnings, conversions, scale, opportunity gained, and opportunity lost and more. It means MONEY! I've worked hard for what I earned over the years and I did it the HARD way. Stupid me.

I didn't have a mentor until I had already made my fortune. The result, poor planning, no checklist and faulty actions. The ultimate result...I lost it all, **not once but twice!**

For me, math has become the final solution and the only resource that has never failed me. Even when it worked against me...because I didn't know how to use it, math was still steady and predictable, wasn't it? That's when I had an epiphany. A light bulb lit up and I came to my senses. I got a mentor and my life, and my income, changed forever.

For you who are a lot like me, I need direction, training, guidance, mentoring and more training. I have always been motivated to achieve more, get more, be more and do more but never had the guidance and direction, the checklist if you will, that I needed.

As an adult learner, I achieved my bachelor's degree, a master's degree and a PhD after I was 40 years old! I didn't earn the PhD until I was 62! Never too old to learn, right? I was not motivated to do all that until I got a mentor and grew up a bit. All from a simple math equation.

Perseverance + Motivation = MY success.

We will move on to another formula that you are going to love. It is simple too. I believe in the theory, the practice that I should work once and get paid over and repeatedly. Do you like that one? Hope so.

Another Formula for Success

Income = Work Once X Pay - Pay - Pay- Pay

"Think, Strategize, Plan, Try, Do,
Do-Again, And-Again, Keep on Doing
and Expect Success"

- Dr. Mark Zupo

*"A gem cannot be polished without friction,
nor a man perfected without trials."*
- Seneca

The World Is Changing to Your Advantage

Kool Stuff ---

Growth:

The top 10 in demand jobs in 2016 didn't exist in 2009

1 in 4 workers has been with their employer less than one year

1 out 6 people married in the U.S. in 2016 met online (Me too!)

There are over 200-million users on Myspace

There are over 100-billion searches on Google every month

It took radio 38 years to reach an audience of 50 million

TV - 13 years

Internet - 4 years

iPod - 3 years

Facebook - 2 years

The number if Internet devices in 1984 was 1,000

1992 - 1 million

2008 - 1 Billion

More information will be generated this year than in all the past 5,000 years

Technological information is doubling every 2 years

By the time a student finishes a 4-year technical degree, what they learned will be outdated by their third year of study

Japan has successfully tested a fiber optic cable that can carry 14-trillion bits of data per second on a single strand of fiber...

That's 210-million phone calls per second...

The prediction is that by 2049, a single $1,000 computer will exceed the computational capability of the entire human species

83-million babies will be born this year (2016)

By 2050 there will be an estimated 10-billion people on the planet

In China, the top 25% of people with the highest IQ's exceeds the total number of people in North America

For the first time in history, there are four generations working side by side. (Traditionalists, Boomers, Genx's, Millennial)

Over 3-billion people use the Internet in 2016

75-billion devices will be connected by 2020

10-million self-driving cars will be on the road by 2020

There are over 1.55-billion monthly active Facebook users

1 in 5 divorces yearly are blamed on Facebook

More than 2-billion people own a smart phone

The game Candy Crush earns about $850,000 per day or $230-million per year

4,000+ new books are published every day (4,001 including this one)

50% of the world's population is under 30 years old

96% of Millennial adults have joined a social network

80% of companies use social media for recruitment

The fastest growing segment on Facebook is 55-65-year-old females

Wikipedia has over 15-million articles

80% are non-English

There are over 200-million Blogs

For the first time in history Kindle book outsold printed books at Christmas 2016

SUMMARY:

Understanding the power of a massive email list. Understanding the power of a small email list and the masses of people you can reach.

Action:

Develop your multiple streams of income. Engage with online customers to build relationships.

Module 7

The Multiple Streams Mastery System™

How to Build an Online Business With Multiple Streams Mastery™

"There is no better time than now to do what you should have done yesterday"

- Dr. Mark Zupo

The first thing one must understand is that I always wanted to be a millionaire. When that statement was made at age 14, the second thing was that I had no idea how I was going to achieve that goal! There is likely a great difference in what I believed success as and what you might believe that success is for you.

The road to "success" was fraught with potholes and barriers and took over 20 years for me to sort through trial and error, experiences, misfortunes and delays without anyone to help or look to for guidance. Today, however, it is very different world. Digital and online opportunity is beyond unbelievable and provides for a multitude of mentors and coaches to look to for help and guidance.

I first became aware of selling online in 1991. I was as green as they come back then. Although I was a bit of an entrepreneur, I had no idea how to transfer that knowledge to the Internet and sell someting online let alone make money from it. There was one thing I did want and that was to learn as much about the Internet and the selling process as possible.

My first online venture was selling a $5 three-page report on "How to Use Your Computer to Make Money!" No kidding! The funny thing was...I didn't even own a computer!

There came a day when I realized that I needed a mentor or coach who had the experience to help me become an online business owner. It was tough to find someone who would help until I met Cory Rudl in 1996. Sadly, Mr. Rudl died in a car crash in 2005. Mr. Rudl was "THE" Internet Marketing Coach of the century. He was also my mentor for one very important meeting before his death that helped me to realize my potential in online business marketing.

Today, I have friends in the industry that keep me on track, focused and provide me with the support and training to maintain my success. And trust me...I lean on them constantly!

My wife, Kathy, is the "go-to" inspiration and unbelievable support mechanism in the process of finding my success online and as a professional educator. My success is the undeniable result of her support and guidance throughout my learning and experimenting experience.

All that she does for me is reflected in my experiences, my endeavors, my products, my coaching platform and my brand..." A Life You Can Count On"!

So, let's talk about where I am and how I realized my own success.

I now know. I have multiple streams of income. Seven in total.

My 7EVEN™ Sources of Revenue

Although there are several more online revenue sources to choose from, I have chosen the ones that work the best for me. I will share the 7EVEN™ that work for me.

Steps in The Process.

1. **Product Creation Launch Revenue**
2. **Coaching Revenue**
3. **Membership Revenue**
4. **Affiliate Marketing Revenue**
5. **Social Media Ad Revenue**
6. **Live Seminar Presentation Revenue**
7. **Marketing Services Revenue**

1. Product Launches: 46%

***NOTE - This is my best predictable revenue generator EVER!**

The mainstay of Internet marketing is one simple standard that I teach all my students...become a product machine! There are four main rules of action associated with product development.

1. Give more than is required.

2. Produce something that helps other people.

3. Produce something of value.

4. Solve a problem.

The conversion from physical products to digital products has dominated the market and will overwhelm most media forms from now on. If you don't adjust to digital media platforms immediately...you will be lost to those with the insight and foresight to improve with the times.

Today, the affiliation between Internet marketers fostered relationships between professionals to promote each other's product to their individual lists and multiply the demand and sales throughout the online communities. A single product launch can generate many thousands of dollars in a single hour if promoted correctly. The simplest model is to presell, sell, post sell and then offer reduction just prior to closing the defined sale period.

2. Membership Sites: 38%

***NOTE - This is my best continuity revenue generator EVER!**

Micro-membership sites have become the newest form of community to evolve in digital marketing and relationship building among entrepreneurs. This form of recurring passive income has defined the new "job" of Internet entrepreneurs. The simplest model is to presell, sell, post sell and then offer reduction just prior to closing the defined sale period.

Every month, income is generated passively as members remain engaged with valuable advice and content predetermined and dripped to their inbox. The predictable income is generated passively based on their willingness to remain members so long as I deliver value. The privilege of membership is supported by access to "secret" or exclusive content designed just for them that non-members do not have access to.

Social Media Ad Revenue: 1%

Another superb opportunity to generate residual income is the ad revenue model. This isn't as productive as other methods but still help to fill the void and helps to monetize my other social media presences. The extra money generated here is better than no money at all! The focus should remain to the greatest method of generating revenue and the least attention should be paid to the ones that don't perform as well. Pareto's 80/20 rule works here well.

Affiliate Marketing: 1%

A great resource for online entrepreneurs is that there is an endless supply of other people's products. Some are not so good, and others are great. It is one of the easiest ways to generate profit from other people who work hard to produce outstanding products. Simply promote someone else's product and earn a commission! Usually all you must do is market their product or service to your list and if it is worthy your followers will gladly buy in and generate income for you.

Some call this affiliate marketing and some call it a joint venture. Either way you can earn handsome profits from the process as well as build trust and authority with your followers. I use my blog, www.MarkZupo.com/blog, to promote such offers through indirect selling. That is referring to the products mentioned and directing other people to see what all the fuss is about.

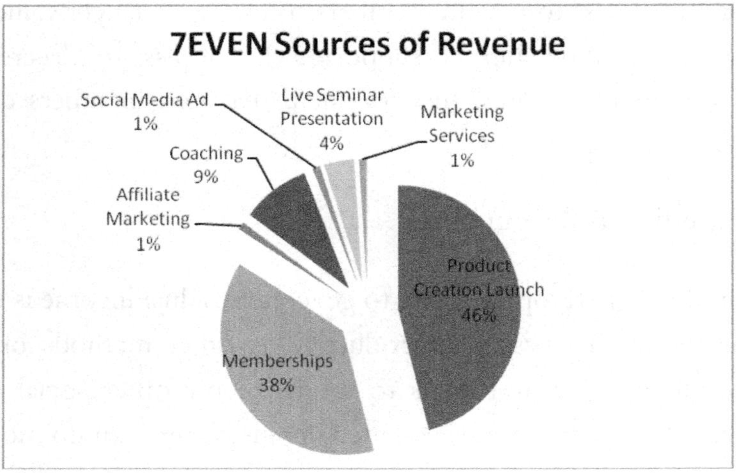

Figure 1. Multiple Streams Mastery Program™
7EVEN Sources of Revenue

Coaching Revenue: 9%

***NOTE - This is my best on-demand revenue generator EVER!**

Coaching is the method of revenue generation that I like the most. It can be daunting though. It requires a great deal of attention to individuals, but it also helps to build relationships and make friends with thousands of super people with like interests. Just like my rules above, it must help people, provide value and solve a problem. I can tell you that there is no greater reward than to see someone that you helped achieve a goal or find their personal success.

Coaching can also be hugely profitable if you spend serious attention to promoting that form of personal growth and development. Some coaches charge huge fees for individual attention and exclusive access. I prefer not to devote all my attention here because it is also the most time consuming for me and takes away from other things I like to do for my students and followers.

Live Seminar Revenue: 4%

***NOTE - This is my best immediate bulk-income revenue generator EVER!**

Live seminars! Of all, this is my personal favorite and the most fun. There is nothing like being the celebrity in performance of my skills and experiences to thousands. However, it also takes the greatest toll on my energy and effort. I am most comfortable in front of large groups of people teaching, coaching, mentoring and speaking to their needs and wants. The personal and up-close attention is a great ego builder for me and I love that of course. As it takes super energy to perform, it remains a small part of my revenue generation because it is time limiting as well.

Other Services: .01%

My experience is in the development of digital and virtual products...one time. The object to maximizing my time and effort is to produce work once and let it produce income ongoing! Passive and recurring.

This is my signature training program.

MULTIPLE STREAMS MASTERY™

17 ways to sell what you know packaged as a product:

1. **Books**
2. **Video Course / Program on DVD**
3. **Audio Course / Program on CD**
4. **Digital eBooks**
5. **Tele-Seminars**
6. **Webinars**
7. **Live Seminars**
8. **Recorded Webinars**
9. **Affiliate Programs**
10. **Joint Ventures**
11. **Fundraisers**
12. **Corporate Sponsorship**
13. **Coaching Programs**
14. **Consulting**
15. **Mentorship Programs**
16. **Public Speaking**
17. **Masterminds**

The Future:

I've spent a great deal of my life helping other people. I've learned a great deal along the way that has made making a living easier and quicker. I still face MANY challenges and obstacles but if I didn't the journey would not be worth the result.

In 2015, I've learned by drinking from the "fire hose" method because I am getting older and my time to help others and myself grows shorter. I will be spending most of my time now on membership sites and developing other modes of recurring revenue in those platforms. For me, the "laptop" lifestyle is the only opportunity I want to pursue.

When I started, I found 114 people who paid me $24 a month for a newsletter / blog and a few PDF's. That's $2,736 a month from a poor blog site with lousy content from a newbie Internet marketer with no list! When I say that I generated this money from nothing, no list, no marketing, no advertising and no email autoresponder, I mean it! Unbelievable, right?

I know it can be done because I did it. I must add a note here to qualify the success I just mentioned. Most if not all those people eventually dropped off and the income went away quickly after about 6-months. I didn't know what I was doing. No mentor, remember? I paid for it by losing the income generator I set up because I didn't build a relationship with them. I just posted occasionally, and it got old for them and the result was that they all left. Predictable, right? And yes...there is a formula for that too!

The best buyers were the 100 or so people that believed in me. If I sold them a $24 service I could have sold them a $100, $200, $500 or $1,000 service as well.

Do the MATH!

I could have done one-on-one coaching at $400 each. I could have done group coaching at $197 a month each. I could have, I could have, I could have... but I didn't.

After 9 months of struggle, I opened my flagship coaching program for $997 a year to each student. It gave them training, webinars, training materials, goals, expectations and access to me. They could pay all at once or three times. If they paid all at once it was $997 a year one-time payment. If they paid three times it was $375 each payment that totaled $1,125 a year.

In the first 90 days, I had 35 people sign up. There were 26 who paid all at once. A nice injection of $25,992! There were 9 people who opted for the three-pay method. Another $3,375 a month for three payments. <u>That totals $29,367 for the first month!</u>

Done right, the laptop lifestyle delivers autonomy with relationship-building at the same time. I have a great feeling for my business and for your business for the new year.

Charge on and make it happen!

"Greatness is in influence, and not necessarily in affluence. It is not achieved by being a 'paper millionaire', but by being a 'people millionaire'."

- Ogwo David Emenike

<u>Summary:</u>

Revenue Sources
Revenue Tracking
Revenue Focus
Revenue Mastery

<u>Action:</u>

Once you have developed your revenue streams, develop tracking and building the profitable ones. Measure your performance and improve it.

PART 3

The Action Steps

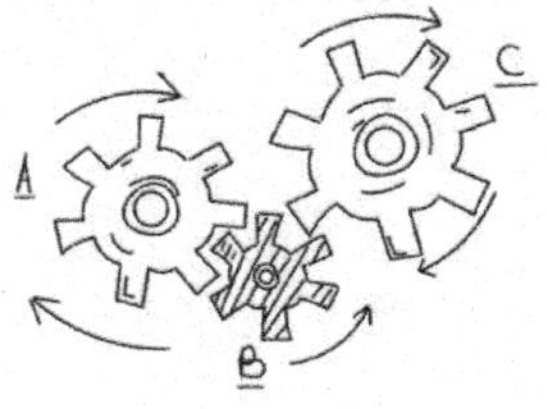

MODULE 8

My Stream Runs Up Hill!

The Magic of Multiple Streams of Income

Multiple Streams Mastery™ Rolled Into One Amazing Opportunity.

Some understanding of where we are today with some simple analogies of the evolvement of communication.

- Morse Code have become the new Smoke Signals
- News Papers have become the new Morse Code
- Radio has become the new Newspaper
- Television has become the new Radio
- Telephone has become the new Television
- The Internet has become the new Telephone
- Virtual Reality has become the new Social Connect
- Social Media has become the new Technology Revolution

We probably don't need to convince you how BIG social media is. But when we checked out these amazing facts and figures, it's truly ASTOUNDING.

Did You Know?

- There are currently 3.419 Billion Internet users worldwide - **2.307 Billion of them are on social media!**
- **In 2016, Facebook has 1.59 Billion users** with the highest penetration and engagement of Internet users at 63%
- Instagram has **400 Million users**; registers the second highest at 27%
- Pinterest has **100 Million users**
- And **29% of online adults use LinkedIn**...

If you thought that was awesome,
here's where things get interesting...

- **Social media advertising budgets DOUBLED worldwide over the past 2 years** — going from $16 Billion in 2014 to a whopping $31 Billion in 2017!
- Social media spending in the U.S. alone is expected to increase to **$17.34 Billion in 2019**
- In 2016, **Facebook brought in $6.8 Billion in advertising revenue** (up from $4.3 Billion)
- **Instagram brought in $1.53 Billion in mobile ad revenue** in the same year
- The number of YouTube channels earning 6 figures per year is up **50% year-over-year**
- In 2017, analysts predict a **26.3% global increase on spending for social media ads**

All I Can Say Is... WOW!

Concentrate on the "masses" of people who will see your offer!

Although I have not verified this statistic, I've been told that a millionaire has generally seven streams of income. The mistake I made when I started out. I had ONE. However, there isn't truth in everything you hear or read. There is no magic formula for wealth and income creation. The focus should be on the multiple forms of income that drive a more secure financial opportunity NOT to lose everything when any one thing goes bust. ---Like what happened to me.

1. Your attention should be learning these key forms.

- Earned Income
- Passive Income
- Recurring Income
- On-Demand Income
- The Lottery
- A Rich Uncle / Aunt (Deceased)

2. There is No Magic Formula.

- Multiply Your Effort by Delegation
- Multiply Your Effort Through Outsourcing
- Multiple Your Effort by Adding Multiple Streams
- Minimize Your Workload by Systemization

Let's explore where you may be and where you want to go. The choice is yours.

Wikipedia: "...The U.S. Internal Revenue Service categorizes **income** *into three broad types,* **active income, passive income**, *and portfolio* **income.** *It defines* **passive income** *as only coming from two sources: rental activity or "trade or business activities in which you do not materially participate."*

Earned Active Income: You work for someone else. You trade time for money. You allow your employer to dictate your worth. Money is highly taxed. Net is a percentage of pre-described charges. You allow your employer to define and control your time, effort, ability, creativity, freedom and independence. (Sucks).

Passive Income: The income resulting from cash flow received on a regular basis, requiring minimal to no effort by the recipient to maintain it. Sounds like the right kind to me. I think you'll like this one too.

Recurring Income: The income that is the portion of a company's **revenue** that is highly likely to continue in the future. This is **revenue** that is predictable, stable and can be counted on in the future with a high degree of certainty. Can I get an **"OH YEAH"** here too?

On-Demand Income: This is a hot one for those just starting out in the online arena. The most on-demand income belongs to the less advantaged people in this country especially. They trade labor (work) for a set amount of pay relative to the work performed. **The "On-demand" pseudo-taxi services are an example of on-demand income.** Basically, temporary and non-permanent workers.

**HOWEVER - I'm going to show you how to exploit this style of income that has produced HUGE profits for some Internet marketers.

The Lottery: Don't even go there. Save your money. The odds are stacked against you. It is considered "the opiate of the masses[1]."

[1] *something regarded as inducing a false and unrealistic sense of contentment among people.*

A Rich Deceased Aunt or Uncle:

A deceased Rich Aunt or Uncle: Start off by thinking about the fact that you are basing your future on that plan. Really?

** A note here - There is no magic pill or process to acquiring wealth, success, independence, freedom or anything else for that matter. There is only a process and system to journey from where you are to where you want to be. My results are NOT typical. Yours will not be either.

There are in fact, some steadfast rules to help you get there, wherever 'there" is for you.

I call them the "Rules of Zupo."

Number 1. You must compound the effort of the single person into the energy of many people.

Number 2. You must maintain your focus without ever looking for "the next shiny object."

Number 3. You must develop multiple offers based on your passion, experience and expertise.

Number 4. You must present yourself in a dynamic way to engage and offer value to those you will help.

Number 5. You must center your effort on a specific niche and not sway from the singleness of mind.

Number 6. You must believe that your offers are timed with the needs of others as there is no better time than now.

Number 7. You must NEVER stop learning from those who have done it before you.

Get a mentor.

Get a mentor

Get a mentor!

There are no magical formulas. There are however, thrilling, exciting and electrifying days ahead if you start to reach for your goals today. Do it because you want it not because I said you need it. Find your "why" and move on it. There has never been a better time, I swear it. You have more tools and resources than any human has ever had up to today.

"Work needs to be hard, exhaustive, laborious, trying, all-consuming, soul-crushing, mind-numbing, creativity-destroying, energy-sucking and inspiration obliterating." …

And that's the bullshit you've been taught to believe all your life to keep you right where you are!

Well, it isn't so, and it doesn't have to be so unless you allow it to be so.

Dr. Mark Zupo

Module 9
Beliefs

"You can only dance with success once you have struggled with failure"
- Dr. Mark Zupo

A Powerful Message About You

I am hardly a writer. I am however an entrepreneur and thought-leader driven by my passion to succeed and understand the power of the passion to succeed. Failure has given me a freedom that is not revealed until quite some time after experienced. It takes time to digest and comprehend what has been lost as well as accomplished. Each opportunity to write and teach is an opportunity to share a multitude of lessons, experience and reason. The first attempt to be read was my first book, " THE ADVERSITY UNIVERSITY™" that detailed a struggle and triumph that took on a life of its own and remains today steadfast as an impactful and dynamic example of my place in the world through my words, my life and my voice.

The most remembered people on the planet are famous for their success and not recognized for their failures. The foundations of legend and legacy are rooted in their success over adversity and triumph over tragedy even though their individual failures may have been epic! That was well chronicled in The Adversity University™ book. Compared to those of us who are insignificant in the world and without recognition for our individual contributions to humanity, we long to admire the successes of others above our own and seek to be recognized globally for our efforts.

There is no-one better suited than ourselves to talk about our individual success than you and me because there is no-one more knowledgeable about who we are and what we have achieved...and how we have failed. To overlook our failures is a shame because it has been the mold for our character, our resolve and our value to others for their admiration, though we may be more recognized for our failures than our successes.

Those we choose to follow and admire as successful people, leaders and mentors, have been more visible in their success than in their failures. The result is an abundance of humility born from an abundance of hardship and endurance. Every baby learns to walk by falling and every entrepreneur learns to succeed by failing...some miserably and in grand fashion! I speak from personal experience, of course.

Let it be acknowledged that your passions, life experience, education and knowledge will be the fundamental spiritual, mental, physical engine that drives your success. The greatest and most radical improvement to your life will be the result of an actionable plan and the purpose of your being. You have a fundamental opportunity to change the world and reality through building a legacy from your life. It is all about:

Who you are

Who you are perceived to be

What you represent to others

What you must do

What you must not do

How you will do it

This is the strategy for ultimate personal success that determines who you are, who you will be and who you were to those that have known you. This is your opportunity for your legacy that will give after you have departed this world. It is not about luck, being born to the right family, advanced education or extreme training. It is about your desire to win, your desire to achieve and your passion to succeed against the challenges that you will face

It is all about how you share your success in the service to others.

This lesson shared promotes the importance of your role in other's lives. It demands your selfless engagement in the transformational message that you share as those shared with you. As I share my thoughts and experiences, my passions and my intentions on social media sites, I am drawn to create my own inspiration from the ashes of my own failures and to share what I have learned in a personal open example of what worked for me in my quest for success and what might work for you in your quest for similar opportunities. This book is the product of my experience, education, passions and dreams. It represents the path I took to my success and a guide for you to your success. The opportunity to be the success you want to be has never been better than today.

I've outlined the key elements to success that only you can apply from where you stand today. ...and the best place to start is from where you stand...or sit...or play...or sleep. The point is...anywhere! This book is written for you to use as a guide for personal success. Read it now to get started, use it while you are working at success and re-read it when you need to reestablish your identity as a success. Action is the key phrase.

NEVER BETTER!

Creating your "life" product and marketing your "life" experience is the most fundamental way of sharing, teaching and improving your life as well as the life of other people.

The one thing that has not changed since I was old enough to believe in myself is that I was worth something more, I was worthy of something bigger and I could help other people achieve their dreams of personal wealth, freedom and independence.

Apply the principles outlined in this book, join my coaching program and or attend my training sessions and discover a wealth of information that will help you share your education, experience, passions and talents learned on your road to personal success. Turn them into products that will reward you for the rest of your life experience.

Ask yourself the most powerful questions and answer them with more powerful responses.

- ✓ What would you do if you knew you couldn't fail?
- ✓ What would you do if there were zero obstacles to anything you did that would guarantee your success?
- ✓ What would your future life look like?
- ✓ Who would you have in your life looking forward?
- ✓ What will you do with your success once you've achieved it?

Let your story of failure and success be a bright light in your quest for success to strengthen your resolve and champion the cause.

Are you still learning?

There are two entities that develop power or impedes power, they are the engine and the load.

If you're not curious, you're not learning, if you're not challenging yourself beyond comfortable limits, admitting your mistakes to capture a learning moment...then you stop creating useful things and become stagnant and the "load" instead of an engine.

My approach to a future of success isn't radical or new, it is just a reevaluation of solid principles that you already know but have forgotten how to use for your benefit.

I believe in the "Nay-Sayers" because they anger me enough to drive me to prove them wrong...and I have done so EVERY TIME!

“When the Student is Ready, The Teacher Will Appear.”

It doesn't matter if you are already rich and famous or you are still searching for your fortune and notoriety, you still can learn how to launch a new persona and catapult your personal development and create a new future for you and your family.

Pure and simple, the rules have changed in just the last few years, in fact they change radically in just the last few weeks! The way we accomplish things and move about our lives is very different since the financial crisis and global threats have entered our vocabularies.

That said, the way we do business has also changed, for the better! The availability of technology, social media connections, virtual relationships and global reach has grown to gigantic proportions.

There has NEVER been a better time than today to redefine your personality, your skills, your offering and your value!

If you think that you should remain a member of the status-quo, you are wrong. A lesson in leadership and direction is in order. Let's talk about the traits of real leaders...the explorers.

10 Traits of Real Explorers

What I think is missing from our life today are the traits of the explorers that have revealed a world of wonder and marvel. We have become small pieces of the big puzzle instead of a part of the big picture! We need to develop and massage the **ten** traits that will make us leaders and successes.

We are experts. We have the traits of leaders and explorers, but they have been quoted by the needs of time and funding. Today we have failed to keep up with the personal and human engine that helped it become the value and the worth we represent to new employers and our careers. As much as technology has benefitted our society, it has also taken away some of our individualism and uniqueness.

10 Traits of Real Explorers

Focus

Creativity

Curiosity

Resilience

Risk taking

Conviction

Independence

Perseverance

Preparedness

A sense of higher purpose

Are you an explorer?

How to Re-Package your Life Experience and Make Your Uniqueness Your Product!

Tell Your Life Story.

Everything we've read about the celebrity's lives on the newsstands for the past fifty years has been negative. From the time, they were kid stars to when they grew old and out of circulation. Your story is just as important and just as exciting...written the right way. It will be a chronological view of your experiences.

My mother used to watch the soap operas every day when I was very young. Funny thing is, one day when I went to see her 30-years later, the TV was on and guess what? I saw the very same people doing the very same things and the very same dialog that I saw 30 years ago! It was a life-story that never ended. That's powerful!

Reveal Your Leadership

As one's life takes place day by day, you demonstrate your authority in many ways whether you know it or not. To share your story, you also share your credibility, trust, influence and your expert status. Regardless of what your expertise is.

If you know anything at all and express what you know to another person, you imply your expertise and your authority. I've lived an exciting life by accident as opposed to by design. My life story is a dynamic read. Yours is too! Sharing your story will command respect and empathy from those who identify with your life's trials and successes. You become trusted.

Every Story Is a Lesson

When others read your life story it becomes a lesson for their future life when they place themselves in your shoes. The foundation of your experiences can become the foundation for a dynamic experience for your readers sharing your breakthroughs, insights, failures, successes and opportunities. Sharing is crucial to building trust and demonstrates the "Before and After" study of your experiences.

How Your Story Links to Their Story

Begin your story from the beginning. Show how you've grown from then to now.

Describe what made you fear success and failure. Explain how you tried to make your passions a reality. Or how you failed to do so.

Describe what worked and what didn't. Express your life-changing moments and revelations.

Share who helped you and who didn't. And why. Explain in detail what your goals and what they are now. Explain your life history as you would a clear and understandable novel.

Write about it, record it, video it, narrate it, be interviewed for it and share it. It means more to people than you can imagine. It builds trust and credibility as well as authority. Live it, love it, Share it.

Summary:

Your story. Your life experiences. What you've learned. How you have helped others. Powerful questions. Beliefs.

Action:

Your story: Write about it, record it, video it, narrate it, be interviewed for it and share it. It means more to people than you can imagine. It builds trust and credibility as well as authority. Live it, love it, Share it.

"It's hard to wait around for something you know might never happen; but it's harder to give up when you know it's everything you want."

- Unknown

MODULE 10

See It to Believe It

Beliefs About Money that can cripple you or support you!

The first step is not to teach you about money but to "un-teach" you about what you have learned about money and the beliefs you've held on to. Subconsciously you believe many things that are important to your life even though you learned them before you could understand them.

Money is one of those things. Most of the beliefs about money are outdated and do not apply today. They came from your parents when you were too young to understand them.

You will have to start all over again and I'll help you find out what you really believe about money and what it means to you now, not in someone else's past.

Let's Unlearn Our Beliefs About Money

We will also learn why it is important to know this now and what it will mean to your future success.

Here are some things we "believe" about money.

- Rich people keep getting richer
- Making money is hard

- Money is the root of all evil
- If I were rich I would share my money
- Money hides from me
- Rich people have more time to make more money
- Money doesn't grow on trees
- My family has always been broke
- Rich people are different
- I'll never be rich
- We've always struggled for our money
- There are no millionaires in my family
- I don't have a rich uncle
- I'd be happy with just a million dollars
- Poor people will always be poor
- The system is designed to keep me poor
- And so, on and so on....

You Control Your Mindset!

To begin to change your beliefs about money you must first change your attitude and mindset.

- Do you believe that money and luck are related?
- Do you believe that people are born rich?
- Do you believe that money changes people?
- Do you believe that rich people are selfish?
- Do you think you can still be rich?
- Do you believe that you'll never be rich?
- What would be enough money for you?
- What are your perceptions about winning the lottery?
- What do you think about overnight success?

- Do you believe in immediate gratitude?
- Do you think rich people are honest?
- What do you think about banks?

The first thing to do is separate your thoughts and answers into two categories; Rich thoughts and poor thoughts. Is your answer something a rich person would say, or a poor person would say?

1. I'm not financially free, because ___________.
2. I'd love to have more money, but ___________.

There are two laws you must know about and how they can work for you or work against you. They are:

Rich Laws and Poor Laws

RICH LAWS:

- ➢ Rich people earn income from money that works for them while they earn more money
- ➢ The rich invest in things that keep or increase their value.
- ➢ Rich people become wealthy saving their earnings.
- ➢ Rich people worked hard for the money they made

POOR LAWS:

- ➢ Poor people will always be poor
- ➢ Poor people want someone to take care of them
- ➢ Poor people believe that other people control their wealth

- Poor people are born to be poor
- Poor people don't know how to handle money
- Poor people waste money

These and other statements permeate the world as un-objective opinions from people who might be poor and people who don't consider themselves poor. What do you think when we talk about poor people? The question really should be...what amount of money, or the lack of money makes one poor?

You might be shocked even by your own response when you start to look at it. The idea here is to understand the correlations between money beliefs and what your opinions are. The answer is to write down the things you want to believe about money that will move you closer to getting what you want.

When it comes to money, real money, experience is irrelevant, and accomplishments are everything. The best example of success is realized at the bank. Period.

People who have money understand these laws and use them to their advantage. Today, the Internet has become the most unbelievable way for the "average" person to capture their "share" of the wealth. Again, here, experience is irrelevant. The real earners, the highest achievers, the remarkable people who earn more than their individual effort should allow. Unless, they are aware of the opportunity that the Internet and online businesses offer.

The law of large numbers – a million-to-one odds happen more than 300 times a day!

When it comes to math and money, both have beginning in the heart. Both require passion and concentration. Both can make or break you physically, emotionally and spiritually. Most people work for someone else, their general belief is one that speaks of needing to be comfortable...but not necessarily security. Most believe that provided they get their check every week or two that they will survive.

Nothing could be further from the truth.
Comfort does not translate into security

They relinquish independence by agreeing to trade their time and skills for pay. The tradeoff is fair to a degree.

Again, nothing could be farther from the truth.

It never ceases to amaze me why anyone thinks it must be that way. When you have a skill or ability that someone is willing to pay you for then you also have a means to independence and the freedom you want too. I think it is important to look for a means to express your skills and abilities to the degree that you decide is a fair trade. Determine what you think your value and worth is worth to someone else. There are relationships everywhere and building relationships is important…period.

When I fail I am not able to be a success. WRONG!

When you fail you can be the next success! We've proven that many times over. I embrace failure and run with it because it means that I have something to correct my failure and strive to be the eventual success. Consider it an accomplishment. Find success in everything that you do...even failing!

What does this have to do with math and success? Everything.

Your experience is irrelevant if you fail to use it to produce something from everything you know. Your resume is a prime example of success and failure. Yes, I said failure. It demonstrates your past successes and will ultimately be used to judge you if you fail to produce. If you fail to accomplish your goals or the goals of your employer, you fail. Period.

It is all about results. It's a formula.

That said, why not produce the results for yourself because who better knows your strengths, passions and resolve to earn enough to help yourself and help others too.

Relationships. Math and life are all about relationships. How you build relationships will directly determine your results. This best example in the online business arena. On the Internet, your relationships will direct people to you just because the perception of you is one of integrity, honesty, respect and trust. You never know what or who you'll find at the end of the extra mile!

Millionaires are masters of building wealth and especially building relationships.

- ✓ Millionaires: Set goals.
- ✓ Millionaires: Don't focus on possessions
- ✓ Millionaires: Invest in themselves
- ✓ Millionaires: Trust but verify
- ✓ Millionaires: Inspect and expect
- ✓ Millionaires: Measure everything
- ✓ Millionaires: Demand more and give more
- ✓ Millionaires: Never fear competition

"In my opinion, it's not about the money. It's about the relationships that the money brings. Without relationships, the money isn't as valuable."

- Dr. Mark Zupo

"What would ~~you~~ I do if ~~you~~ I had start all over again?"

Here are the ten most important things I would do if I were to start over again today!

1. Commit myself to focusing on an Online Internet Business from today on.

It is up to you to decide whether you will trade your time for money or start a business that pays you what you are worth. Establish it and work it until you drop working a nine-five J.O.B. ever again. You immediately MUST believe in yourself and your determination, resolve and intent to succeed no matter what.

2. Begin reading and digesting every motivational-inspirational book on the market written by Internet Marketing Experts!

When I started reading way back when, I knew that I would do something big but didn't know what it was. I was motivated by successful people and decided that I would be one too. Your state of mind is critical to your success. Adopt a never quit attitude. Embrace a success or success mentality no matter what. Find every personal development guru and know them better than they know themselves!

3. Pick the hottest market niche immediately.

When I started my venture into Internet marketing, I thought that everyone would want my products, and everyone would buy everything I had. Wrong! I failed to ask what the customer wanted. Critical...no less. What do people want? To be healthy, lose weight, look younger, know more, avoid pain, have more relaxation, remove stress, find love, be more fit...and more. That's where I would direct my focus immediately.

4. Focus my attention and every part of my being on learning everything about it immediately.

I would devote my remaining life on the study of this market. I would learn every aspect of its life. What drives it. Who needs it. Where I can apply my personal focus to it. Study the competition. Find the experts. Visit them. Ask them everything. Make it mine.

5. Select the proper business model and stick to it no matter what.

My personal business model is to build a list. Develop an advertisement. Drive traffic to a landing page. Collect their email address. Send people from the landing page to free training. Then a webinar that has a front-end offer which ultimately leads to a high-ticket back end offer. **(HINT – My Million-Dollar business model)**

6. Stat building a list immediately.

If I were a Genie I would go back in time and build, build, build a list. It will pay you handsomely and continue to support you when times are tough. That happens sometime. I would do it from day one and never stop even after some success. This is the one lesson I learned up front and it has paid off ever since.

7. Set up and use Social Media Facebook ads immediately.

Facebook! What can I say. Well, I can say that today it is the absolute best marketing platform for the money ever. That may change but for today it screams profits! If I had been aware of the power of paid traffic marketing back when I would have begun paying for it and conditioning myself to spend my money on it the very first thing. With Facebook, $5 a day does it for each campaign. You can increase the amount as your earnings allow. Believe me, I wouldn't stop at $1,000 day! Condition your mind now to spend what is necessary to get your message out there using social media paid advertising.

8. I would ignore my critics and "Nay-Sayers" immediately.

Anytime someone acts it draws attention. Sometimes good and sometimes bad. But the criticism you will get is to be ignored. The action always brings money. So, take the good with the bad and IGNORE the bad criticism. Once your success is recognized you will magically be sought after for your expertise and commended on your action-taking guts. Stop caring what other people think of you. It is you that is important. It is what you think that is important. It is what you do that is important. Build thick skin. The more money you make the greater the criticism. Use it to your advantage. It is verification that you are reaching people! Can I get a Yeehaaw here? ...***YEEHAA!***

9. Develop a no-lose mentality immediately.

If you quit, then your dream quits. Your intentions quit. Your desire quits. Your passions quit. That isn't what you want or what you started this for is it? No. NEVER QUIT. NEVER QUIT. NEVER QUIT.

Filter out the things that won't work early and often. Then get to work on what will work immediately thereafter. You will fail sometimes but that is a learning lesson on how not to fail that way again. Thomas Edison found 10,000 ways a light bulb won't work. He also found the one way it does work. Nothing else need to be said, right?

10. Surround myself with energetic and like-minded motivational people immediately.

A quick story. When I was 10 years old I was told that I was stupid. I was told that I could never learn anything because I was stupid. I was told that I would never be anybody important because I was stupid. If you hear it enough you will soon believe that you are stupid, right? NO.

I was not stupid, and I was going to prove it someday!

Someday came after some failures and failed attempts to prove it to myself too.

I attempted college. Three times.

HOWEVER!

I went on to start my own business and made my first million before I was 32 years old! Can I get an OH, Yeah here? Oh Yeah!

I still had a burning desire and wanted to prove I wasn't stupid and making a million dollars wasn't good enough.

My environment was a gathering of wealthy people because when you have money you become recognized for your money in this world.

They all were educated, and I wasn't. It didn't matter because I was wealthy, but I still wanted to prove it.

I went back to college at 40 years old.

Got my first degree. Took five years. So, what!

Went back and got another higher degree. Took three years. So, what!

Enough is never enough for me. I am driven.

Went back to college and got a Doctorate in Education. Took six years. So, what? No...

Now I have accomplished what I wanted to and proved that I am not stupid!

Now I am surrounded by the most educated and intelligent people in society. People who seek me out to ask my advice because...I am not stupid! I surround myself with the brightest and super-successful people in the world. I am fortified and recognized for my passion, my success and my education every day. It is uplifting.

You can do the same. Just do it. Never quit.

Your message of success will get itself out even when you aren't paying attention to it. Be inspired, act, focus. Continue learning and improving every minute of every day.

The purpose of this exercise is to help you understand that there are steps to take when you start a business and after you fail at business. The point is to HAVE A PLAN OF ACTION! No matter what. The best thing you can do for yourself is to surround yourself with people that can and are willing to help you avoid timely and costly mistakes.

Summary:

Money. Starting over. Beliefs. Plan of action. Genius moments. Personal business model.

Action:

Develop your personal business model. Put together a plan of action. Write a bulleted list of actions and expected results.

Part 4

The Opportunity

MODULE 11

Building an Online Business With Multiple Streams of Income™

I always wanted to be a millionaire. When that statement was made at age 14, the second thing was that I had no idea how I was going to achieve that goal! There are misconceptions about what I believed success was for me and what you might believe that success is for you.

The road to "success" was fraught with potholes and barriers and took over 20 years for me to sort through trial and error, experiences, misfortunes and delays without anyone to help or look to for guidance. Today, however, it is very different world. Digital and online opportunity is beyond unbelievable and provides for a multitude of mentors and coaches to look to for help and guidance.

I first became aware of selling online in 1991. I was as green as they come back then. Although I was a bit of an entrepreneur, I had no idea how to transfer that knowledge to the Internet and sell someting online let alone make money from it. There was one thing though that I did want and that was to learn as much about the Internet and the selling process as possible.

My first online venture was selling a $5 three-page report on "How to Use Your Computer to Make Money!" No kidding! The funny thing was...I didn't even own a computer!

There came a day when I realized that I needed a mentor or coach who had the experience I needed to help me become an online business owner. It was tough to find someone who would help until I met Cory Rudl in 1996. Sadly, Mr. Rudl died in a car crash in 2005. Mr. Rudl was "THE" Internet Marketing Coach of the century. He was also my mentor for one very important meeting before his death that helped me to realize my potential in online business marketing.

Today, I have friends in the industry that keep me on track, focused and provide me with the support and training to maintain my success. And trust me...I lean on them constantly!

My wife, Kathy, is the "go-to" inspiration and unbelievable support mechanism in the process of finding my success online and as a professional educator. My success is the undeniable result of her support and guidance throughout my learning and experimenting experience.

All that she does for me is reflected in my experiences, my endeavors, my products, my coaching platform and my brand...the "Math of Success Master" of the 21st Century!' I know it's korny but....

So, let's talk about where I am and how I achieved the success I now know. I have multiple streams of income. Seven in total.

THE GOLD! The MAP!
The Blueprint!
The PLAN
The Whatever You Want It to Be!

The math is simple…
build a Million-dollar Empire that
You Can Count On!

A. The Choice is yours.

1. Determine your wants and needs.

The PLAN: Monthly Membership @ $97 per

The Math: $97 each

100 members

$9,700 per month

$9,700 X 12 = <u>$116, 400 per year!</u>

B. The Foundation: Your Book @ $20 Each

The Math: $20 sales X 100 per month

100 X $20 = $2,000 per month

$2,000 per month X 12 = <u>$24,000 per year</u>

C. Platinum Membership Sales @ $495 per

The math: $495 each

100 X $495 = $49,500 per month

$49,500 per month

$49,500 X 12 = <u>$594,000 per year</u>

D. Seminars and Webinars

The Math: $2,000 each

100 X $2,000 each = $200,000

$200,000 X 1-time per year = $200,000

$200,000 X 2-times per year = $400,000

possible IN ONE WEEKEND!

E. Coaching

The Math: $500-$5,000 each per

7 members

7 members per session / per month / per year / per whatever

The opportunities are endless.

7 X $5,000 = $35,000

$35,000 X 12 = <u>$420,000 per year (+/-)</u>

F. <u>Total - $1,354,400!</u>

You can put in whatever numbers that you feel comfortable with. Change them up, move them around. The deal is that you can determine what your sales and profit can be. It's up to you. It's your choice. If you do any part of this you are ahead, right? What would an extra $5,000 a month do for you? An extra $7,500 a month?

There isn't any guarantee that your success will mirror mine or that you can achieve even the smallest figures in this formula. It is for example purposes only and your results are determined by your own effort, experiences, education, resolve and more.

It is a simple formula to start you thinking. ...And working on it. Nothing happens until you start doing something. So... Do It! See what you come up with.

More - Traffic
What if you had 100 people a day visiting your website or viewing your product and services online?

100 people a day is more than realistic.
100 people a day visit
(if your count them for 30-days a month that adds up to more than 3,000 people a month!) But we'll stay with the low numbers to be realistic and conservative. The low numbers still excite me, how about you?

7 people a day join your information-based blog or newsletter that entices them to buy something or get free information. They submit their email address to access anything.

3 people a day buy your entry-level product
3 people a day X $24 - $37 = $72 - $111
1 person per month becomes a member
1 X $495 = $495
$495 X 12 = $5,940 per year

--- Of the 12 people per year that join, at least 3 may buy your premium product @ $5,000 or $25,000. **Do the math!** It all adds up to more than you're making now, right?

No matter how you count it. If it even comes close to $10,000 a month that's $120,000 per year! Are you making that now? Do you want that now? YES!

How accurate are those numbers and estimates? They aren't specific, and they are changeable to your needs, wants, desires, effort and more. Sometimes the number of people is less and sometimes they are more. It is just for an example to start with.

Not everyone spends, stays or remains engaged. Not everyone trusts you or believes that you will deliver. There might be someone who spend $34 and then opts for your premium program at $5,000 or $25,000 or $100,000! You never know. That's what makes this fun. Try to figure out what didn't work and trash it. Try to figure out what worked and REPEAT IT! The variable is as endless as the possibilities.

Imagine...just 100 people. WOW.

What frustrates you?
What excites you?
What do you want?
What do you need?
What turns you on?

In my opinion, Membership Sites are the single-most productive way to start and produce the kind of results that will excite you.

We've discussed the reasoning earlier. You build it once and reap the profit passively, recurrently and essentially, ...forever. They perform continually. They provide everyone with a place to feel as a part of something that is really meant to help them, to be a part of a community. And... you can sell it later when you tire of it for even more money!

There are some basic benefits to membership sites that you need to know about. They are:

They can be operated from anywhere on the planet where an Internet connection can be made

There aren't any physical products. Everything is digital 24/7

You can operate it with simple tweaks from time to time

You can build relationships through it with simple personal touches

They are low cost to start up and low cost to maintain

They can provide reliable, passive, recurring income forever if you so choose

The process can be huge fun

They can provide you with celebrity status and credibility or authority

They can be hugely profitable

Obviously, it is, in my opinion, the best, foremost and only startup anyone should consider. Period.

Choose your niche, your topic, your focus and run with it.

So, how can you do this? Read on...

The: **Multiple Streams Mastery Membership Program™** is the best strategy for building and growing your own profitable membership platform.

Here's how it works:

This program is a three-day training program.

> **Day 1 -** Building the Blueprint Day for your personal membership platform. Here is where everyone starts! This is an extensive ground-floor training day. It's exciting and rewarding all in one. The first day is a presentation of the steps and everything you'll need to know to get started immediately setting up your membership site(s). This training is universal for very form of membership site. You'll choose the one best for you and your goals.

> **Day 2 -** The Meat and Potato's Day to discover the membership model you like best to meet your goals. On this day, you'll also meet the community of other membership entrepreneurs. You'll learn the pros and cons of different platforms and models. There are many of them and you'll summarize all of them for you. We'll look at real-world case studies and other membership experiments that have failed and been very successful. You'll learn the best methods, trick, systems, platforms, insights and

techniques that have made ours successful.

Then, you'll join our community and you'll learn how to create your own. A thriving membership community is, "money in the bank." You will build relationship that will drive your business. You'll learn how content will be the MASTER of your community. You'll also learn how to outsource and use surveys to maintain your community wants and needs.

Day 3 - The "Ka-Ching" Day to learn how to profit from your membership site. You will learn how to monetize your membership site. How to collect money on a recurring and passive basis. How to structure your site for maximum profit and ease of management. How to give away a membership for 'FREE" and still make money. Then, how you continue to repurpose your membership site to make additional profit. You'll learn about reciprocity, community, relationship-building, monetization, launching, marketing and more!

PLUS! - The newest funnel-building techniques to attract and build a huge mailing list. This new feature has become a critical part of Internet Marketing and Membership Site Success.

Where the rubber meets the road. I have a PhD in education. It's great to be called:

Doctor Mark Zupo. It cost me $120,000 and six years of my life! What came with it? Nothing but debt and no guarantees for future success. I spent 13 years in college and have never made a dime from it. PERIOD!

However, I have more than 25 years in the Internet marketing arena and have a great deal of success to show for it. There are no guarantees that you will be successful. My income claims are for education purposes only. My successes are not typical. BUT, if I can do it..........well you figure it out.

To hire me personally to mentor you as a consultant would cost you more than $5,000 a day. That's what 25 years of experience costs. That's also why it isn't affordable for most people and why I offer this training at reasonable prices and the opportunity for everyone to learn from my mistakes and successes.

So, that said, I offer this 3-day Online training regularly for $5,000. The seminar format will cost you $10,000! Believe me when I say that there are many people itching to enroll right now. Of course, space is always limited which allows for the demand and respective pricing.

When I offer the seminar training I promise that it is worth every penny and more!

Watch for it.

That's why I now offer the training Online for the exclusive reduced price! Isn't that what you really wanted to hear? Yes, of course.

This is a drastically reduced price for my exclusive members only. It will not be repeated. I've reduced it by a whopping 85% below what others will pay.

Act today.

Enroll ASAP or lose this once-in-a-lifetime opportunity to change your life and find the independence and freedom that you've been searching for.

Make a commitment to me today and I'll return the favor and make a commitment to you.

Here's where you can access the finest training, for less than you think, for the exclusive one-time membership site training and recurring income stream.

This training will sell out fast and there are no guarantees you can get in until next year at a higher price. OR...maybe not at all if we don't offer it again. I don't want to turn anyone away, but you may not be able to get in if you don't act now.

You can waste years of valuable time and precious dollars on simple mistakes that you'll make without this exclusive training.

So, enroll now before it is too late.
Keep in mind...the Multiple Streams Mastery Membership Program isn't about building income as much as it is about building a passive recurring income stream.

The final opportunity:

1. Fast start-up procedures

2. Blueprint Guide

3. Formats and Platforms

4. Systematization

5. monetization

6. Members and Relationships

7. Regularly priced at ~~$5,000~~, ~~$2,000~~, ~~$1,200~~

8. *NOW ONLY* $429

This price will be increased soon!

Hurry! Enroll Now!

Your Uniqueness
is Your Product!

Here are 15 ways to sell what you know packaged as a product:

Books

Video Course / Program on DVD

Audio Course / Program on CD

Digital eBooks

Tele-Seminars

Webinars

Live Seminars

Recorded Webinars

Affiliate Programs

Joint Ventures

Fundraisers

Corporate Sponsorship

Coaching Programs

Mentorship Programs

Public Speaking

Charge on and make it happen!

Your New Life Story
I Am, I Can, I Want to.
I Should, I Could, I Will, I Do.
- Dr. Mark Zupo

Summary:

Multiple Streams Mastery Program. Training. Mentorship. The product "You". The blueprint. The map. The goal. 100 people.

Action:

Enroll now before it is too late.

Keep in mind...the Multiple Streams Mastery Membership Program isn't about building income as much as it is about building a passive recurring income stream.

MODULE 12
WHAT IF?

What If you had a one-million-dollar business?
Let's do the math...

What If?

A million-dollar business, that's about $20,000 a week for 50 weeks, right?

What If? ...
You had a million dollars. How many people could you help find their success?

You could pay all your bills and rest confident that you don't owe anyone?

You could give you family all the things they have sacrificed without for years?

You could run the million-dollar business from the comfort of your home or while on vacation, at the coffee-shop?

The Multiple Streams
Million-Dollar Formula™.

The formula lays out my personal $1-Million training formula.

The Multiple Streams Formula™

The very formula I developed ***after*** building my business to one-million dollars ***after*** losing everything to Bankruptcy and Foreclosure, the expense of Cancer treatments and the Business Mortgage crisis of 2008. Yes, it can be done, and I've proved it.

So, I guess you've seen other people making a fortune, right?

...and you've said to yourself, "If he / she can do it so can I"., right?

...and why am I not making the kind of money he / she is making?

...and am I not smart enough, am I not worthy enough? WHAT??

...and what if...?

- **Well, what if it is possible for you to have the money you deserve?**
- **What if you did make a million dollars next year?**
- **What if you could show everyone that you were smart enough, you were deserving enough?**

What if?

What if it IS possible for YOU to take in $1 million dollars in one year?

Let me tell you that you are deserving enough, and I believe in you! I believe that you can do it.

BUT ---

- ✓ You must believe it too. Do you?
- ✓ Do you believe that you are deserving?
- ✓ Do you believe that you can do it?
- ✓ Do you believe that you have what it takes?
- ✓ Do you believe that you can meet the challenge?
- ✓ Do you believe that you are just as capable as anyone else?

So, it doesn't matter if I believe it however it **ABSOLUTELY MATTERS** if

If...you believe it!

A very rich guy once told me the most important thing I have ever learned years ago after I told him that, "I wanted to be a millionaire". He said, "Mark, you can do anything you want in life first, as long as you get other people to believe that you are genuine in your intentions and you firmly believe that you can do it". Second is that you look the part. If you want to be a millionaire, you should look like a millionaire to be believable.

With that, I took all the tips I could get to "look" like a millionaire. I dressed differently, talked differently, acted differently and presented myself differently. I became a millionaire before I ever made a dime.

...and I was believed once I made an impression in other people's eyes.

So now, I'm going to share how I made that possible.

I'm going to show you how you have kept yourself from ever earning a million dollars in the past and how to **change that mindset immediately!**

Ready?

Let's get started, Here's the formula.

Using an analogy. Let's go to the grocery store.

Step 1: First, find a need. When you discover you are out of something or going to be out of something you make a mental; or paper note to get it, right?
The List.

Step 2: Then you make time to make the run to the store. You delegate time to do it, right?
The plan.

Step 3: You ensure that you have your list, a coat, the gas and the time and you...go, right.
The Travel.

Step 4: At the store, using your list, you methodically move through each aisle until you find what you need, and you collect it in the cart.
The Tools.

Step 5: Then you move to the cashier, pay for it and move outside to

your car to get it home.
The Action.

...and so, on and so on.

Well, making a million dollars is **JUST LIKE** that. It doesn't happen all at one time. It takes some planning, training, decision-making, tools, effort, action and more.

Simple, right? I know, you and I both know that it is more complicated at the same time.

Well, not so when we break it down like this.

$1 million dollars is also $20,000 fifty times.

$1 million dollars is also $50,000 twenty times. About the amount of the average salary in the U.S.

So, if you got paid $20,000 every week for 50 weeks, you would have about $1 million dollars, right. Let's look at $20,000 broken down in smaller increments. Easier to understand and apply to your situation.

If you had a consulting or coaching business that you worked from home and charged:

$20,000 a week. Don't think you can? WELL, it is being done every day! There are people doing it every day all day long. Here's how.

Imagine that you had several (multiple) streams of income

from one business. like a -

$100 Online training program

$500 Group coaching program

$1,000 Exclusive Membership Program

$5,000 Mastermind Group

Add it all up and presto! $20,000!

Still feel like that's impossible? Let's break it down some more:

$100 Online training program	= 200 buyers	= $20,000
$500 Group coaching program	= 40 clients	= $20,000
$1,000 Exclusive Membership Program	= 20 clients	= $20,000
$5,000 Mastermind Group	= 4 clients	= $20,000

It gets easier to believe, doesn't it? That's how many people do it. Don't you believe that you can too with the right training, effort and energy?

But where do you start?

But where do you get training?

But where do you learn the method, the system, the pros and cons?

There are people who use Facebook ads for their $5,000 programs.

There are people who use Google ads for their leads generation.

There are some people who rely on Youtube for their video traffic generation and some...use other methods of traffic generation to make it happen for them.

"Just the Facts Maam".

Some of these works and some of these don't. Some of these things work for some people and some of these things don't work for others.
It's a numbers game of trial and chance. Too risky for me. (And you).

There's a better way. A simple formula to train, track, traffic, teach and tell and then...profit! A system. My system. **The Multi Streams Mastery Formula**™. It's simple and to the point. Easy to follow and concise. Reliable and systematic. A business system for you to follow.

The BEST business in the world are the ones without any moving parts. The one's where they are digital or electronic and automatic, right?

So, with that in mind, wouldn't it be best for you to put your effort in a business like that? In fact, you could even make less and be happy, right? Sure, you could. Every time you report for work and stare at the clock for 8 hours, right? So, let's examine this a bit further.

What if...you started to think of better ways to do this.

You're a mathematician.

You're already entrepreneurial.

You're thinking like a millionaire already!

You see, many people fail to ever accomplish a goal of making a million dollars more because they don't think like a millionaire and they do not act like a millionaire. Now you now have the basics for the formula already and it is to focus your attention on one of the five possible steps I mentioned earlier.

Just one will do it, right? YES!

The top earners in the world do ONE thing and focus their absolute attention on that ONE thing and they do that ONE thing very well. You are now thinking that you can too, right. Yes, I am right, and I know it.

Don't be fooled though, it takes hard work, ingenuity, massive effort, undying devotion, some risk and complete focus.

- You will need advice.
- You'll need training.
- You'll need foresight and intuition.
- You'll need to drive traffic and conversions.

and most of all, a coach who will help you change your thinking. Especially about price-points! Here's where you give an OH Yeah!

Price points. Instead of struggling to get:

Reverse-engineer it into simpler terms…

$100	Online training program	= 200 buyers	= $20,000
$500	Group coaching program	= 40 clients	= $20,000
$1,000	Exclusive Membership Program	= 20 clients	= $20,000
$5,000	Mastermind Group	= 4 clients	= $20,000

Why not attract those same people ONCE A WEEK!

A lot simpler, right? YES.

So, let's look at that scenario:

How about 1 sale at	$5000	= $5,000
How about 5 sales at	$1000	= $5,000
How about 10 sales at	$500	= $5,000
How about 50 sales at	$100	= $5,000
GUESS WHAT?		**= <u>$20,000</u>**

Instead of struggling to find buyers at a higher price-point, you focus on smaller increments which equals the same $20,000?

Doesn't this excite you? It should. **Wahoo!**

Isn't this a better opportunity?

Isn't this possible?

The ultimate question is, "can you believe that you can do this now?" **Say it! ……………. YES, YOU CAN!**

What would this mean to you? What would this mean to your family? What would the next 12-months look like for you as compared to the last 12-months? What would the next 12-months mean to those around you if you made this happen.

HOW BAD DO YOU WANT IT?

Don't just take my word for it. DO THE MATH. Work it out for yourself. Make it make sense.

If this is what you want, look me up. My **Multiple Streams Mastery Formula™** has worked for me for the last 20-years. I believe in it.

Summary:

How bad do you want it? Think like a millionaire. Price points. A better way. What if? What would this mean to you? What would this mean to your family? What would the next 12-months look like for you as compared to the last 12-months? What would the next 12-

months mean to those around you if you made this happen.

<u>Action:</u>

Contact me for the **Multiple Streams Mastery Formula™ and the Multiple Streams Mastery Program Training™.** You will need advice, training, foresight and intuition, traffic and conversions.

> …and most of all, a coach who will help you change your thinking.

MODULE 13

HOW TO FAIL SUCCESSFULLY

"Ignorance + Inaction = Failure
Action + Failure = Experience,
Experience Plus Action = Success"
- Dr. Mark Zupo

There are 7 Reasons Failure Can Boost You to Success

The key phrase is reason. There isn't anyone who understands failure like me. We can look at the famous failures in the world and use their models for success through failure to guide our management style, our home life, our business life, friendships and our personal and professional lives.

Forrest for the Trees

One doesn't have to look far to find successful failures. Not everyone we recognize as successful arrived there at the end of a well-planned journey. Often, the most famous examples of success faced huge obstacles and roadblocks that was the catalyst for their recognized successes. As is demonstrated in every form of academia, the smartest people are not often the most successful people. A degree does not guarantee success. For example, I made a fortune long before I ever had a degree.

Some of the most well-known people in the world were also some of the least-well known for their failures;

Henry Ford: The road to success for the automobile guru failed into bankruptcy five times in other businesses before he founded the successful Ford Motor Company.

Walt Disney: Today, Walt Disney is the icon for family and fun in movies, theme parks and merchandising. However, he was a complete failure as a newspaper editor and fired because he, "lacked imagination"! Go figure....

Abe Lincoln: Abe failed miserably at politics and his military career. He went to war a captain and returned a private only to become president. He also failed in business seven time to include bankruptcy and social embarrassment. Yet he is known as one of this country's greatest leaders.

Bill Gates: A college drop-out, Gates failed at data businesses again and again until he founded Microsoft. And the rest is history. One of the world's richest men, Bill Gates embodies all that we consider as success. But born from failure.

Albert Einstein: The term genius is synonymous with the name Einstein. Yet Albert Einstein didn't speak until he was four and could not read until he was eleven! He was expelled from school, shunned and ignored as well as considered an abject academic and social failure, handicapped and anti-social among his peers and educators. Yet he was later awarded the Nobel prize for physics and recognized as the father of modern physics. Put that in your pipe and smoke it!

.and more.

The Key to Failure

The key to our retort to failure is the key to our success. Failure has benefits if we consider them an ally instead of an adversary;

1. Failure gives opportunity to learn.

The opportunity to learn is a valuable teacher when we seek to blame others for our failures. Originality is frequently born from a lack of experience.

2. Failure demands accountability.

The failure to change can be a fatal flaw in our perception of the need to learn from and move forward. Making mistakes means you are doing something. Not making mistakes only translates to a reluctance to change based on what we learned from our failures.

3. Failure is a reason to explore.

The highest prize for failure is taking a grasp on the reason we fail and seeking another avenue to enhance our success. To investigate the motive is to explore the weakness and seek to overcome it.

4. Great Success is born from great fear.

Success comes just beyond your comfort zone. Fear usually propels one to **success** just after you have experienced what seems to be insurmountable fear. Rejection, disappointment, setback, defeat, and soul-crushing denial are the murderers of success.

5. Mindset sets the stage for success.

There is no greater tool in the arsenal of success-building than mindset. After all, who can control one's success better than you? A healthy mind can deliver the crushing blow to defeat again and again. The roots of the greatest success develop from the seeds of overcoming adversity and defeat.

6. Failure demands change.

It once was said that, "our failure to learn from our defeat will demand that we repeat our future poor performance." Change is essential to demonstrate that we have learned from our mistakes to not repeat them. The slightest delay in change will cement our feet to collapse and guarantee our failure. Memories and habit are formed by connections from positive experiences. They are strengthened by repeated experiences and success.

Podcast, Blog, and Media...Interview Opportunities upon Request
Go to: InterviewDrMarkZupo

Failure is reason for improvement.

Improvement is always the intuitive result of innovation when directed by the experience of failure. No greater examples of innovation are aerospace travel and aviation where the experience of failure has written the rule book of future success.

The sweetest victory are the spoils of the tough battles. With this, I say that we need to embrace failure with the same enthusiasm as we embrace success...and then model our efforts thus so.

I have the formula for my success that I follow to the letter. It is an exacting 7-step process that I detail in my Multiple Streams Mastery training. They are simple and easy to remember steps as well as an easy to implement "recipe".

The Multiple Streams Mastery Success Program™

1. **Generate**
2. **System-mate**
3. **Automate**
4. **Duplicate**
5. **Designate**
6. **Delegate**
7. **Replicate**

"A sure-fire formula for failure -
Fail to ask your clients what they need and then fail to give them what they want."
- Dr. Mark Zupo

Work is defined as:

...The application of incremental instances of energy and effort towards your goal.

MY definition of work is defined as:

"...The use of initial energy to develop the exact systems, techniques, tools and automatic processes used wisely as the investment in myself up front to produce recurring, passive income forever"

Summary:
The keys to failure. Successful failures.

The program for success

7-Steps

Options

MPI - Find Your Massive - Passive - Income

Action:
Be reasonable. Understands that failure can be used as a tool. Look at the famous failures in the world and use their models for "success through failure" to guide our management style, our home life, our business life, friendships and our personal and professional relationships.

MODULE 14

IT'S ALL GONE!

"Those people noted for their success did not achieve it because of revolutionary opportunity, they were granted it because of extraordinary effort"
- Dr. Mark Zupo

That was a terrifying moment for me just a few years ago when I sat in my car and realized that I had lost everything I had worked 30 years for! Gone, bankrupt, foreclosed, repossessed, forfeited, and forevermore GONE!

I'll explain.

When I met my first wife, Kay, we were young, impressionable and eager. It didn't take long to welcome my son into the world. He was born exactly 9-months to the day that we were married. He would be Mark Jr. Seven years later my daughter, Traci, was born. My family was perfect. Gorgeous, well-behaved and smart kids with a level-headed, smart and gorgeous model wife.

As an entrepreneur, I was making good money for the time. More than most grown men were. Life was good, and we took it all in. My kids were growing up smart, happy and good looking. In 1992, my handsome son, Mark, was killed in a car accident. A drunk driver hit him head on about three blocks from the house. Life changed immediately.

I became despondent, hated everything and everybody. It is hard to explain unless you've been there. It took more than ten years for me to calm down and get my head out of my ass and join the rest of the world again.

My wife was never the same. We seemed to play at life with little emotion injected. As things got somewhat better, life would change again.

About ten years after losing our son, my wife would be diagnosed with Cancer. Oh no, not just any Cancer but an elusive, extremely rare sort called Pseudomyxoma Peritonei. Not only rare but always fatal. …and in short order. No treatment, no cure, no nothing but the eventual reality of death!

Kay would die a miserable, painful death about six months after her diagnosis. Comatose for more than a month before. She wanted to die at home and her wish was granted. I stayed with her, never leaving the house, for 40 days and nights until the end.

I thought I had control of life when I was young. I didn't. Not even close.

There I was, 50 years old, widowed, insurance poor, broke, bankrupt, soon to be homeless, a failed business due to the economy, no income, no job, no real education and corporate experience and more.

IT WAS ALL GONE. 30 years of hard work, planning, saving and expecting that the world would treat me as well as I had treated it. NOPE! NOT!

They took my house, my savings, my credit, my retirement, my rental properties, my cars, my business, my dignity and my pride.

"I was breaking in every way imaginable…physically, emotionally, financially, psychologically, in my relationships, my credit, my trustworthiness, my authority and more."

- Dr. Mark Zupo

It was also a crucial moment for me as I was successful businessman, successful negotiator, practical financial investor and savvy entrepreneur. ...or so I thought! What I didn't count on was that I really didn't have control of anything if someone else had control of my ability to earn. Namely, the real estate market and the government's ability to level...and I mean "flatten" the ability of millions to make a living by the swipe of the pen.

I made a commitment to myself from that moment on that no single individual or entity would ever have that kind of control over my financial future like that again. I also had to find a way to level the playing field so that I could recover in the least amount of time possible.

In this Module, I'd like to highlight on my thoughts and lessons learned from my experience with a few short-term tactics. The tactics, strategy and techniques that made me whole again. Tactics you can use as techniques to help you build an online business and grow your social presence.

To put it all in perspective...I lived at a garbage dump for several years as a young man. Yes, you read right. A GARBAGE DUMP! That said, there was no place to go but up. Right? I always sought-after riches because that seemed to me to be the vehicle that would propel me from the dump to the real world where I would be accepted as "someone".

THE BIG PICTURE

"The one thing that you can always count on is that you can always count on just one thing...YOU."

- Dr. Mark Zupo

Along the way from poor and uneducated to reaching my first million dollars, I had a mentor that always focused my attention on the BIG PICTURE. It seemed far away most of the time as my earning were incremental and small compared to the wealth I so hungrily sought after. But it wasn't the jobs I was doing but the people I encountered along the way!

The lesson here is: Relationship-Building

Any man or woman that relies on themselves for education, guidance, support, training and coaching is missing a key ingredient in their success...other people who know more and are willing to share their expertise!

My first real found success involved a real estate expert who was willing to mentor me. For a price, of course. But he did so willingly, and his guidance was the key factor in my becoming a real estate investor and making more than $1-Million dollars in real estate! Can I get an ...."OH YEAH!"?

The one thing I know and recognize is that I need a coach, mentor and supporter of someone who knows more than I. A critical lesson. Even though I firmly believe that there is nothing I cannot do, really. I believe that with my whole heart. However, I also know that I can do anything, if taught, mentored, coached and guided to the absolute success that experience delivers, even if it isn't my experience.

So, that said, "Go forth and multiply your success." Find a mentor, coach or guide who knows more, has been there and has done that and then SUCK EVERY MORSEL OF KNOWLEDGE FROM THEIR BRAIN. and...do it for yourself!

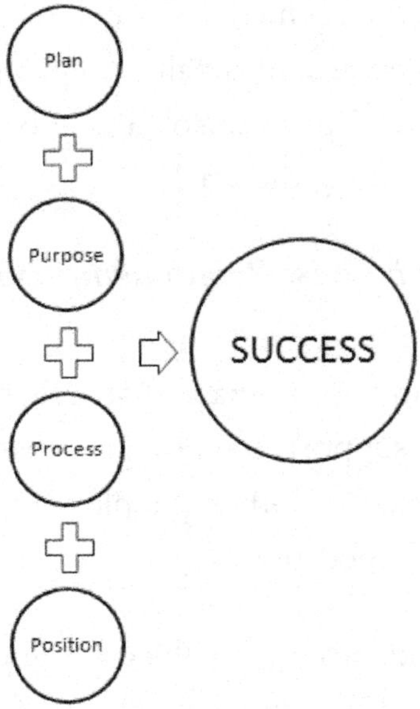

Figure 2. Diagram of The Success Illustration to formulate a plan and action scenario.

➢ 7-Steps to Create You Multiple Streams Mastery Program That Will Change Your Life.

When I was 20 years old I was married and had a son on the way. More importantly, I had no real job. More important than that, I didn't want one. What I wanted was to be an entrepreneur. My new wife had other ideas, so I found a J.O.B. The only thing I could get was working in a restaurant or a manufacturing plant. I chose to go to work in a steel mill.

Bad choice.

I was paid $1.10 an hour for dangerous and miserable work. It was when I saw a man get crushed under a six-ton steel plate that I said to myself, "I'm "outta" here!"

I knew my potential and knew my passions would take me to a better place. That said, I started a new entrepreneurial business and began raking in the cash. Let me state something here.

Multiple streams of income are NOT three J.O.Bs. I was selling potato chips, teaching flying, installing door peep holes in apartment complexes and more. None were passive. All required labor. However, an entrepreneur was born, and I was taking in almost 20 times what I was earning in the mill along other low-paid laborers.

Since then and specifically in the past 20 years I've started and run three very profitable businesses while using the exact formulas that I teach today to other entrepreneurial "wanna-bees." I've since added a total of seven (7EVEN) streams of income. More but for this example we will stay with seven. (remember I said that I like the number 7).

An additional stream of income has become more than merely a luxury but a necessity in today's economies. The goal of almost everyone is to find their personal security, freedom, independence and value even better when they can accomplish that whilst engaging their passion.

Diverse income streams have now become crucial to mere survival for a family today and a barrier to financial ruin, bankruptcy, foreclosure and worse. When your safety, security and freedom rely on one single source of income, it is a gamble that you will maybe lose. Why not insure your safety, security and freedom when you mitigate the risk with The Multiple Streams Mastery System?

In a previous Module we discussed three forms of income:

Earned, passive and on-demand income. You can determine which of the three or combination of the three to engage but, it has become necessary to diversify income streams for your ultimate financial safety. Diversification will help to protect you from major losses in a single industry or downturns in any market. A hard lesson I learned in 2007. I lost everything, too much to go into here but the sum was several homes, cars, an airplane, my credit, my business and more. All steeped in a single industry. The one that failed completely, and I lost it all again!

What you will learn in school is to know about the world, economies and people, art and science, basic mathematics and literature.

What you will **never** learn in school is what to do with it all to stay safe, be prepared, increase your value or help others to do the same!

Fortunately, it isn't any kind of magic. It is rather a formula of simple techniques, training, education, experience and mentorship.

Let's discuss the basics:

A. Build a secure (or secure as possible) initial form of income. Even if it is your current job. Break the return on your investment down to its lowest form to understand everything about it. Work, time, effort divided by pay = net. Divide the net into months, weeks, hours = your satisfactory acceptance of your value to the "company." Determine if it is worth it to you...not to them.

B. Simplify your distinctive value. You have passions, gifts, skills, experience, education and abilities and more importantly...AN OFFERING. (by the way, your offering is the most valuable thing in your tools for success). What you do with your value is what can make you successful, respected, recognized and sought after.

You can be highly paid just for what you know. When you provide your expertise to others, it might seem simple to you but be recognized a hugely valuable to others. Your uniqueness, your personality, your presence, your insight, your passions, your willingness to share with others is a commodity highly prized and eagerly paid for.

How you package your "Product You" determines your success. How you deliver your unique views will determine your success. How you support your offering determines your success. You must be the product..." YOU."

There are many examples all around you. Your doctor, your lawyer, your baker, teacher, firemen and women, pilots, engineers, secretaries, furniture-makers and many more. They all have a unique offering and they all charge for it. Some more than others. The key here is what they (or someone else) thinks they are worth.

Your choice is to determine what you think you are worth! Successful people have something you don't. Skills, experience, education or training. They all perceive that their worth equates what the economy will pay for it. What you will pay for it. So... why not determine what people will pay you for your skills, experience, training, education and more?

C. Identify Your Niche Market. What are the solutions people are looking for that you can offer? An initial action is to determine who will buy from you or better yet, who needs you. Who can you serve the best and what will you charge for that service? Who will pay you for the value you present? What problem can you solve for whom? Who can you help best?

D. Build Community and Relationships. One of the most valuable assets you will ever have is something you can't touch. Your new way of thinking is that your email list now has become one of the most important assets you will ever own. It will be a tool, a security blanket, a friend, a partner and a bunch of other adjectives once you build a list of followers, subscribers, members etc. It is the "holy grail" of tool for every marketer. In the appendix, there is a list of tools and resources that I use.

Note, that I am an affiliate for all of them. I earn a small stipend from them every time someone buys their service through my links. HINT - another income source for me! I use AWeber as my auto-responder program. It works for me. I like it. I use LeadPages for my landing page generator. It works for me. I like it.

E. Create a Unique Product. One of your deliverables can be a free report to help build your list. A newly written report that defines a problem and suggests solutions. It can be an eBook with detailed instructions. It can be an audio with PDF script teaching what they need to know. The idea here is to get a person's email address to access the information you provide.

F. Develop solutions to specific problems. The BEST way to determine what people want is...wait for it...wait for it...to ASK THEM! Once your community is built, quiz them, query them and just plain out...ASK THEM what they want. Then supply the answers. If you can't find the answers, then ask someone who knows the answers and engage as a joint venture with them. This is like a test that you already have the answers to...without cheating! Lol.

Hire a mentor!

Hire a mentor!

Hire a mentor!

I can't strive this enough. A mentor can destroy your learning curve and save thousands of dollars in costly mistakes and wasteful time. I have paid my mentor more than $5,000 a year just to be able to ask a few questions over the phone. However, the return was **ten times** as valuable to me and my business as a result. He paid for himself many times over. Find a mentor, hire a coach or some other form of support person. Do it virtually or in person. Whatever you feel comfortable with. Just DO IT! (Shameless plug here, YES, I am a mentor and coach). (Shhhh but tell everyone you know!)

G. Market, Market, Market! Every single company you have ever heard of, big department stores, manufacturers of toys, home building products, doctors, lawyers, sports teams, celebrity movies and more have used the media to promote themselves or their services, products etc. Look at cereal companies advertising. Baby-boomer medical devices, pills, treatments, retirement facilities and burial services, exercise equipment, jewelry, hair product and products if you don't have hair and want it!

They plan to launch it and advertise that they plan to launch it. Then...they launch the sale of it. Then, they offer a second chance to buy it. Then they offer a special time to buy it before it runs out. Then they discount it when people slow their buying it. And so on, and so on, and so on.

H. Ready 3-2-1 Launch! Look at your favorite company products and follow the steps. It is utterly amazing how they build a relationship with the customers then sell the "H" out of them. It becomes an event that everyone wants to be a part of. Why, HE-double-LL I don't know why but it is!

So, follow the leaders. Follow the successful leaders. Follow the successful, experienced leaders. Follow the successful, experienced, trained, educated leaders who have paid hundreds of thousands of dollars to psychologists, marketing gurus, copywriters, sales people and others to make billions in their industry.

Learn how to launch!

So, Okay, work this. Learn how to build your unique product or service or solutions and launch. Do it one step at a time. Do it now. Start now. The benefits of entrepreneurial success can be huge. Security and freedom is a product of training, coaching, mentorship, action and measurement. Specifically, from a step by step methodology, a plan with goals and actions.

Specifically, through:

Multiple Streams Mastery™.

"Every 9th year I became a failure.
Every 10th year I became a success.
I have taken this path three times.
I never fear failure because it
ultimately leads to success.
It works for me.

- Dr. Mark Zupo

MODULE 15

CALL TO ACTION

"If the facts don't fit the theory...
Change the facts"

- ALBERT EINSTEIN

Don't You Ever Get Tired of Being Poor?

Do you ever feel like all that you do is try and try but never get anywhere?

Like you are...trying too hard,
searching forever,
reading this and that,
listening to other people who have made it?

Trying what they tried but you still aren't getting any real results?

The newest way to market is through the Internet to the masses of people, billions of them but you need something to sell to them and a system to make it all come together, right?

- What you really need is to stop hoping for a miracle
- What you really need is . . . direction, clarity, mentoring and support.
- What you really need is to find the system that works for you.
- What you really need is the answer to your prayers.
- What you really need is the exact system made just for you to succeed
- What you really need is someone to help you do it without breaking the bank
- What you really need is...**a mentor.**

I always rely on writing things down to make things clearer. I make a list of wants, needs, must haves and dreams. I first had to understand the primary concerns before wanting to be rich or famous or wealthy or have credibility and authority. Once understood, I could drive forward with certainty and intention with:

1. **Energy**
2. **Effort**
3. **Expectation**

Try it for yourself and see if it works for you too:

1. The **first** exercise

Describe what you think you really want. Be specific. Write a short three sentence description something like:
I want to stop worrying about my bills, so I can begin to relax and not be so stressed anymore.
I want my kids to have good things instead of second-hand-me-downs.
I want a secure roof over my head.
I want to be an independent entrepreneur by 2018 and beyond.

2. Write out what your life would look like a year from now if you had the one thing you are wishing for. If you won, the lottery or got an inheritance from a rich uncle.

What would your life look like?

How would that make you feel?

How would your life be better?

How could you help someone else's life better?

Now . . . for the ***second part*** of the exercise:

What would happen if you are continuing
to do the things that are NOT getting you greater income because you ***DIDN'T*** get any more money:

Now, what's the difference between number 1 and number 2?
Do a fair job at this, be honest with yourself, this is your private exercise.

So . . . what is the difference?

Do you want to keep doing what you are doing . . .
or...have you conclude that a change is necessary?
SO...

Are you ready to start something new and exciting that will change your life for the better?

If I never learned anything, trying to become successful has taught me that there were rules. Rules that would help to stifle my effort, retard my enthusiasm and reverse my opportunities. The most valuable lesson took over 30-years to learn. And that is:

Don't try and follow the rules. Don't even acknowledge them. Break them before they are made!

"I break the rules that haven't been made yet!"

- Dr. Mark Zupo

Jump on it today. Start today. Take a chance today.

There has never been a better time than now.

- ✓ What would an extra $100 a month do for you?
- ✓ What would an extra $500 a month do for you?
- ✓ What would an extra $1,000 a month do for you?
- ✓ What would an extra $3,0000 a month do for you?
- ✓ What would an extra $10,000 a month do for you?

"If you haven't made any mistakes today then you haven't done anything today"
- Dr. Mark Zupo

There are ways to build and maintain a business today and avoid the ills of yesterday. Specifically, the best near-tern example is the Great Recession of 2007.

Those dark days are over, and a new prosperity is waiting for you to dive in and reap the rewards of entrepreneurship. Now have all the tools and resources that past entrepreneurs didn't have. The marketing world and online business will never be the same. That's a good thing for you! Small business owners have changed to the times and resources however, the rules have not changed nor the fundamentals of business. It still takes endurance, personal sweat-equity investment of time, commitment, resolve, training and new online skills.

A plan of action and specific achievable goals still reign as paramount to your plan and blueprint for success. I've put together, from experience, 7EVEN steps to help your online business grow and succeed:

Never work without a plan and checklist. As a commercial pilot, I don't leave the house without a plan and a checklist.

Be flexible in your planning to confront new barriers and obstacles. It happens. Can change with the 'wind".

Get a Mentor!

Get a Mentor!

Get a Mentor!

Check your ego at the door and learn to listen. Be accountable, be resolute and be available to expect and inspect. Be prepared to blast past your comfort zone. Someone once said, "A tree that doesn't grow dies." Commit yourself to win and never quit. Follow through. Remain accountable. Check your emotions. Its business not personal.

Track and measure everything. What gets tracked and measured gets managed. If you're not aware of what's going on than someone else will be. Develop your systems. Track them, manage them, measure them. Check your returns daily. Check your expenses daily. Check your actions daily. Check your cash flow DAILY! Never invest more than you are willing to lose.

Delegate, relegate, system-ate and follow up! Inspect don't expect because you will always be disappointed. Use future goals as incentive to charge on. NEVER QUIT!

Find the Internet and use it! Live it, love it and use it. Appeal to the masses. It's a numbers game. The more you reach the more you sell and build relationships with. The Internet is ultimately the most powerful tool in your arsenal today. You can touch thousands, millions in a flash. Never fear competition. Your competitors are waiting for you, embrace them and make them customers too!

Embrace the business of NOW. It is digital, virtual, electronic and entrepreneurial. Get on the wagon and hold on for the ride. It will be scary and fun at the same time. Remember to embrace what you earn from your efforts, record, measure, rinse and repeat! Make business fun, be an entrepreneur, make it work for you. You can make it happen for yourself and start today.

"The best day to start was...Yesterday"

Dr. Mark Zupo

Secret Formulas

Momentum:

Momentum is defined as the strength or force that something has when it is moving and the strength that allows something to continue or grow stronger and faster as time passes. It is defined as the mass in motion!

So, what do this mean for you?

Your Action

Your Decision

Your Opportunity

Leverage:

Leverage is defined as the **action** of a lever that pivots about a point and is used to move an object by force applied. It is the advantage of power gained by using an **action** to influence people, events, decisions to an advantage!

There is huge leverage using the math I have described in this book to your advantage. Take for instance, the sheer number of people you can access and help just in the U.S. as well as the world alone.

Current estimates from the U.S. Department of Commerce state that there are:

- **$327 Billion dollars spent online in USA**
- **$3.45 Billion One Day online purchases record in 2016**
- **$1.195 Trillion online purchases Worldwide**
- **$4 Trillion online purchases by 2020**

So, what do these numbers mean for you?

Formulas to Play With

Start a membership site:

Get 27 people to pay you to belong

Charge them $37 dollars a month

That's $999 a month!

That's $11, 988 dollars a YEAR!

Start a blog:

Monetize it with 10 sponsors.

Charge the $100 a post to advertise their product

Recognize them in each post or every other post twice a month.

That's $1,000 a month

That's $12,000 a YEAR!

Start a podcast:

Monetize it with 2-4 sponsors.

Charge the $300-800 an episode to advertise their product / service

Recognize them in each podcast or every other post twice each episode. Times 10 episodes a month. That's $$5,000 a month! (avg. $500 per episode) That's $60,000 a YEAR!

Start a coaching business:

Monetize it with 2-20 clients. (up to 20 if digital)

Charge the $497-$20,000 per month or year.

Times 10 episodes a month.

That's $5,000 a month

That's $60,000 a YEAR!

Your Action

Your Decision

Your Opportunity

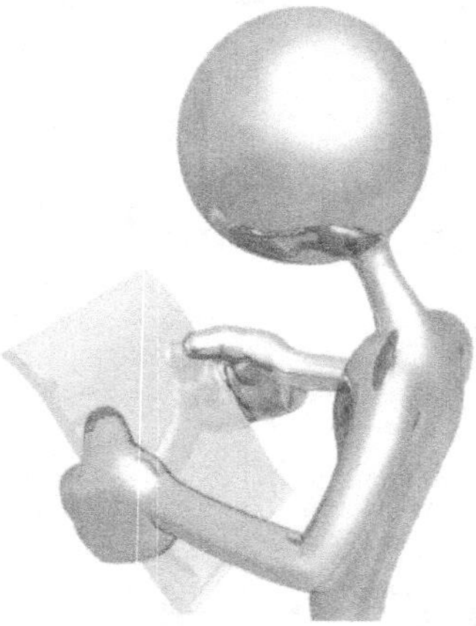

If you have never accomplished the one thing you have always wanted to in life until now –

Read this personal letter from Dr. Mark:

Announcing my Brand New

Personal Mentorship Program:

The Multiple Streams Mastery Program™

MSM

Multiple Streams Mastery™

The Ultimate Passive Income Formula

"The quality of your success relies on
the power of your authority,
the stead of your commitment,
and the exercise of your actions."

- Dr. Mark Zupo

Read this personal letter -

From: Dr. Mark Zupo, Internet Marketer

To: You...IF you are tired of watching others make big bucks on line while you make little or NOTHING.

A question, what frustrates you about your ability to earn a living? Are you frustrated because you are not having the success you have dreamed about online?

Is one of the things holding you back an inability to see the eventuality that you know some of the parts of what to do, but for some reason when you try to do things, they don't all fit together, or work the way they are supposed to?

Are you frustrated because you have been working hard to make money online, and working long hours, but do not have much to show for it?

Are you frustrated because every time you buy another training that promises some new "secret" that it is just some teaching with a new angle to it - but nothing new?

Have you tried system and system, program after program, and they all end up the same way - without making you the money you know you deserve?

Are you tired of buying product after product, learning one new technique, only to find that you need "just one more" to have success?

Does it anger you that there are folks online selling three click-riches programs that just flat-out don't work?

Are you frustrated with trying tactic after tactic and technique after technique only to not make the kind of money you've been dreaming about?

Are you living the life you desire?

If not, let me ask you this: **why not?**

You are online, searching.

You have likely wasted good, hard-earned money on products or trainings that have not gotten you the results that you want. Was it: a fancy, exaggerated up sales letter that promised you that in just a few days, you would know all the secrets you needed to make all the money you ever wanted? Yeah, I know the page. I've been on those pages many times and wasted many dollars for simple answers.

Moreover, it's not your fault. Or mine! I've bought trash like that. So, have many thousands or millions of others. In fact, did you know there are people online who make a living just selling products to people who will never get results?

That's right. In addition, many times those products are empty - not literally, but in their meaning. Because you can study 10 hours of training, watch videos, read tutorials - but you know how it is, you get to something you don't "get", and you are stuck. You literally CANNOT implement what is taught unless you ask a question. However, you hit reply to the email you got from the seller and no one responds. Or, they tell you to submit a support ticket to some firm in India. (Nothing against India, but hey, can someone making $2 an hour in India really tell YOU how to make $100k here?) Right?

There are some specific steps that must occur to make money online. If all the elements aren't in place, you probably aren't going to make money. Period.

Building an online business is much like building an offline business. For example, if you were to open a sandwich shop, what would you need?

You would need:

A location (preferably one where there is a lot of traffic out front during lunchtime)

A good sandwich recipe.

A toaster oven.

A cold case.

A refrigerator.

A cash register.

A few employees.

A method of telling people you are open (advertising, signage, etc.)

If any one of those elements is missing, you aren't going to be making money.

If your sandwiches are no good, no one's coming back.

If you don't have a cash register and a person to take the payments, you won't have money coming in.

If you don't have a location or advertising, no one is coming in to buy sandwiches.

And... It's the same online.

You need:

A location (a website)

Something to sell that people wants to buy.

A delivery mechanism for delivering that something (either postal system if selling a physical item, a digital download system if selling information)

A marketing mechanism (meaning a way to tell other people that you have something of value that is convincing enough for people to pay you)

A way to take money (merchant account, shopping cart, etc.)

If any of these is missing, you aren't going to be making any money.

If you are trying to sell something no one wants, you aren't going to make sales. Unfortunately, I see too many people come into online marketing with an idea that is cool - but no one wants to buy it. In addition, they spend their time trying and trying to talk people into it, but still no one buys. Why not just find something to sell or teach that others really want to buy?

If you don't have a website so people can find your product, if you don't have a way to deliver it, if you don't have all those pieces in place, you just aren't going to be making money online.

So, what about you?

What piece is missing for you?

Are you in the wrong niche?

Are you selling something no one wants?

Or maybe you have something everyone wants, but you are doing a lousy job of telling them about it. Maybe you have a lousy sales page. Maybe when someone joins your list, your email campaign is lousy. Maybe your emails turn people off instead of turning people into buyers.

So, what is it?

What is holding you back from the online success that you want?

You can blame the bad training you have received.

Nevertheless, the fact remains - if that training didn't teach you each of the components I just shared with you, then of course it didn't work.

It doesn't matter what the sales page said, or how strong was the guarantee.

What most people need to be able to figure it all out is something they can ask questions of.

Someone they can get on the phone with and ask questions.

Someone who is there when you get stuck.

Imagine if you could get on the phone once a week with a coach and ask questions about whatever you are working on this week.

Maybe you are writing a new sales letter, but you are stuck trying to figure out what to write.

Alternatively, maybe you know a new niche, and you've 3 different keyword tools and you just can't figure out a niche.

There are things that sell and things that don't. In addition, no matter how many keyword searches something has, if it doesn't sell, it doesn't sell. What if you could talk with someone personally about your idea before you wasted money promoting it?

Imagine if you don't know how to put a squeeze page together and you could get live help to do it.

How about how to create your product or sales funnel?

Or how to write an email campaign?

How would it feel to be able to get on the phone with a real live coach, someone who makes a full-time income online, and someone who is in the trenches doing the work, just like you want to?

Would that make a difference?

If so, you are going to love what I propose next.

Because that is exactly what I am - a personal full-time marketer. I'm not one of those people who say he makes a million dollars a year sitting on the beach doing nothing. I don't. They don't either.

Your best way of learning is to learn from someone who does what you want to do.

I do.

Here's what I do:

I have a time-tested proven system for getting people from starting out to making $1-Grand or $50-Grand a month selling information products.

I have a squeeze page that convinces people to become subscribers.

I have a sales page that convinces people to enroll in coaching.

I have a weekly telephone call that people like you can call into and talk with me personally and I can work with you personally to help you build your business.

And I have a powerful email campaign that strategically convinces people to invest with me.

That's what I do.

It is my system.

It works.

I don't have any other source of income, outside of this online business.

And I can teach you to do the same.

From home. From your laptop. From a coffee shop. While traveling.

That's what I do.

My entire business is on my laptop (and no worries, it is backed up on remote servers as well :-))

So, I work from home sometimes.

I work from a coffee shop sometimes.

I work while traveling sometimes.

But always on my laptop (or once per week on my cell phone for the live weekly call I hold).

Is this what you want?

If so, I can teach you. You want this, right? YES, you do!

Now, one of the things I teach my clients is to have a simple system.

Meaning: consistent traffic, a consistent squeeze page, a powerful email campaign that you write once, a sales page to sell your information, a coaching program so people can ask you questions.

That's all.

If you want something more complicated, go somewhere else.

Sorry, that sounds harsh. It's not. Just the truth.

So, my system is simple.

I don't upsell, down-sell, and cross-sell, beg, plead, cajole, sell your name, lie, cheat, disappear, pawn you off to a low-wage third-world company, or anything else like you've seen other people doing.

I simply teach you my system.

And I make myself available, so you can ask all the questions you need to build your business.

If this sounds good to you, I am going to make you an offer that will change your life if you take me up on it.

And if it doesn't, opt out anytime.

That's right: here's the way it works: you pay a monthly fee to work with me. If at any time you aren't getting 100% value from my training, I'll refund your last payment, and cancel your training. So, what that means is, you can get started today, study for 30 days, talk with me 4 times, and if on the 30th day, you want out - just let me know. I'll refund your money and cancel everything.

And one more thing: there are no guarantees of income. No wild testimonials of freak individuals who "made $1 million dollars working with me in 22 days." with a big FTC disclosure about how this is "not typical results". Well of course, that's not typical results! It has probably NEVER occurred before.

"If I had nine hours to chop down a tree,

I'd spend the first six hours sharpening my axe.'
- Abraham Lincoln

If you are looking for get rich quick, this isn't it. I'm not for you.

Because making real money online isn't 3 clicks and make a million.

No! It takes time. The first month you figure out what you are going to sell and maybe start creating it.

The second month you start building a list and selling to it.

The third month you make more sales and start scaling things.

It's not realistic for it to happen any faster than that, no matter what anyone else has told you.

But let me ask you this, if in the next 3-6 months, you could radically change your life and get on the path to success selling information products and offering a little coaching, would it be worth it?

Would that make a difference in your life?

What would be different?

How would it change the way you live?

The way you travel?

The way you relate to others?

If it would make a difference, let's get started today, shall we?

Successful people tend to be highly focused, and work on a few very specific things that get results for them.

That's why I am very focused about my traffic, getting it from just 2 tight sources.

That's why I am very focused about what I sell - I only sell what I know will give my clients results. Period. I get requests all the time to promote this, promote that, but I don't want to promote anything that doesn't get results. And that's one big reason why I've created so much of my own training - because I've been so utterly disappointed with most of the training out there.

Or maybe you are frustrated because although you know how to do these things, when you go to do them, you get stuck.

The truth of the matter is this: you need a coach.

You need someone who can look at what you are doing and give you laser-targeted direction for the exact next thing you need to do.

Then you go do it.

Then you come back, and he gives you the next step, the next exact laser-targeted step to take.

How would it feel, to have someone take you by the hand, and show you step by step - as you need it, not all in one big brain dump, exactly what to do next, each step of the way?

Would it feel good, like, yeah, I can really do this?

That's what working with me will be like!

Here's the thing - you've been struggling because you've been trying to do it on your own. And you don't want to continue down that path, do you?

In fact, I think that's why you are reading this - because you want to change your life once and for all, right?

You want to finally make things happen online so that you have the success you deserve.

Here's the thing - I don't know what you want for success.

It might be $3000 a month, it might be a million a month.

And you can do either. What kind of income do you need so that you will be able to write your own ticket for the future?

What would that really mean for you?

Would it mean that you could take your family on a one-month vacation anywhere in the world you want to go?

Would it mean that you could pay off all your debts so that you never must owe anyone anything anymore?

Or would it mean that you could give more to your church, or to people who have less than you?

Is there someone or a people group that you really have a heart for, but you just don't have the money to spare right now to help them?

How would it feel to be able to give an extra $1000 to your church from time to time?

What about to give $1000 to a needy family in your neighborhood, how would it feel to be able to just give them a $1000 from time to time to really help them out?

How would that feel?

Would it feel good, like, I'm glad I was able to finally do this?

I talk to people all the time who tell me that they are "intermediate" or "advanced" marketers, but they just aren't making any money.

Maybe…

You know all the steps. You could tell someone else what to do and how to do it.

But when it comes to you - and you go to get started today on building your business - you go blank. You're unsure what to do next.

Does that sound familiar?

The web has changed a lot in the last few years. There is an overload of information online.

And it's becoming a bigger and bigger problem online these days, because as there is more and more information free for the taking, you have too much information and it just creates more confusion.

It would be like learning how to swim or do karate or snowboard, and instead of having one person telling you what to do, there are 50 coaches standing on the sideline, simultaneously screaming out what to do next. Anyone would get utterly confused and overwhelmed.

Read this carefully:

You probably already KNOW more than enough to build a real business, the problem is, that you don't know which part of what you know is relevant to you.

And until you have someone personally show you which part you need for YOU - then you may never reach your goals online.

The truth of the matter is this: it's not a lack of information keeping you from making more money right now.

You probably have hundreds of hours of training on your hard-drive right now.

But it doesn't.

Either because you don't do it right.

So, if information isn't the answer, what is?

Why aren't most people making money online, when there is more information than ever before ready for the taking?

Some of my clients are.

Some of my peers are.

What's different with these people?

Why aren't most people making it, including you?

One reason is that they just don't know what to do.

I know people who make anywhere from 10k a month to 1 million a month. They know what the next step is, every single day when they wake up in the morning . . . and they do it!

Let's face it, even with hundreds of hours of training on your hard-drive - you STILL don't know what you very next step should be.

(Each day you should know the EXACT next step you need to take to grow your business.)

Confusion is what many people are teaching in the programs you buy, and it is NOT what they themselves are doing to make a living.

"The best way to guarantee your success is to demand it"
- Dr. Mark Zupo

So, what's the answer? Read This:

People that sell a claim that a push-button 3-click program that guarantees instant riches are screwballs who will take your money and run. They will deliver nothing that they themselves tried, worked or succeeded at. They make their money selling a system that appears easy, but the opposite is true. They aren't making money from the system they're making money selling you the system. And... that downright sucks.

Feeling sick yet?

You should be.

It's just plain wrong.

It's plain old stealing.

So, what about the other end of the spectrum?

Maybe you've bought a $5k or $10,000 program and you were sorely disappointed. It wasn't outright fraud like the $100 example above - but there was so much complexity and work involved that you just didn't follow through. And when you asked for help, no one wanted to help. Because he already had your money.

Look, if that's happened to you, you are probably feeling angry right now. You see, that's wrong too.

So, what's the answer?

It's so simple, yet for most people frighteningly difficult to do.

You see, to make an income online, make a real, fulltime, income, you need a very special mix of ingredients.

You need traffic.

You need an entry-level product to sell.

And you need a coaching program.

And you need them all in a very special mix.

Too much of one and not enough of the other, and you'll fail.

The mix is critical.

How would it feel to be able to crank out $100k in the next 12 months online?

What would you do with the extra money?

How would your life change?

Here's the thing - I have the mix.

I know what works.

I know what doesn't.

The fads don't.

Buying more products doesn't.

I don't say all this to brag, but it's the truth.

And although I have boiled it down to a formula where you can buy the trainings and just listen to me teach it to you, I have found that my clients that get the most results talk with me personally each week.

That's right.

No matter how much training someone buys from me, their big breakthrough is their first coaching session with me.

That's where the real work gets done.

It's where the real breakthroughs happen.

And that's why I have created this brand-new coaching program, so that you and I can work personally together to get you those breakthroughs.

And when you work personally with me, I push you to get to the next level, whatever that is for you. So, if you are at $0, the goal might be $3000 a month. Or if you are already at $3000 a month, the goal might be to get you to $6000.

But the key here is that this is individualized. You aren't going to get one of those cookie-cutters, where everyone does the same thing. I won't promise you that you will make $100k in 3 months nonsense "systems" that don't work. Look, I can't promise anyone any level of income.

I'm going to push you.

I am going to push you to be the very best.

To get to the success you deserve.

It will change your life.

Once this process frees you of your day job, then you can really dig deep and scale your business as big as you want.

You can choose to just drive more traffic and make more autopilot sales.

Or you can choose to go big and coach others at big levels (imagine the people you can coach when you can tell them you made $$xxx your first year with the system).

What would an online information business mean for you, personally?

Think about it for a second.

Would it mean that you could take a longer vacation this year?

Maybe your wife could quit the job she hates?

Maybe your grandchildren can go to a better college, where they really want to go, not just, where they can afford.

What would it mean for you, personally?

Would you be able to give more to your church?

Pay off your home early?

Travel more?

Really, deep down inside, what would it mean for you to have your own information business this year that is profitable??

So, what about YOU?

What would it mean for YOU?

Would your life go from "working a job to working a dream"?

Would it reduce stress in your life?

Would it make life easier in your family?

Would it allow you to help more people?

Would it "provide your family with stability, income, less worry, and options for education that would not otherwise be possible?"

Would it "open up the path to a much more comfortable life and help you teach your children the value of dedication?"

How would YOUR life change with more income?

With my help you CAN get there, you can make the money you deserve.

Take the next step. Do it NOW!

Get started with me.

Get on the phone with me for your first coaching session.

You will have a breakthrough by the end of the first session.

Then we will meet for 50 more hours through the course of the year.

Teaching you, pushing you, directing you, molding you, giving you the exact answers, you need to build a thriving information business.

It won't be easy. If you want easy, go buy another $100 training program, or another $EXPENSIVE real estate course. Easy doesn't work.

It will be hard work.

I will coach you and guide you through the steps.

And you will do it.

And you will have another breakthrough.

So, what is all this training worth?

Let me ask you this -

What SHOULD I sell it for?

You see, the knowledge is in my head.

But the truth of the matter is that not everyone has the success I've had.

I'm what they call "not-typical"

I've had results that are "not typical" See my earnings disclaimer.

And the average person just doesn't get results like this.

And I don't know how hard you will work, or the results you will get!

But let me ask you this, would it be worth a few hundred a month to gain complete financial freedom and change your life completely?

How would your life change?

Would you feel like you have really accomplished something, like you have done something you could be proud of for yourself?

Over and above all the money, would it be personally satisfying to achieve success, to be able to say you "did it"?

My heart smiled when I read what Dave sent me yesterday:

"And some people responded that they were actually looking for what it was that I had suggested. So, it's like the pieces are already built-in. It's just a matter of me putting it together in a way that gets it 'market ready'. Sometimes I have trouble staying on task.

"Not having a "boss" makes it easy to get sidetracked and procrastinate. As a result, I'm not reaching my potential. I think winning the contest for the chance to work with you, under your guidance, would change all that."

You can do it. And you need my help to take you every step of the way.

Get started with me today, if in 30 days, you haven't had the most amazing experience ever, and are not absolutely blown away by my training, get your money back.

That's right - get started with me today - and not only will I give you your money back if you aren't blown away in the first 30 days - instead of one big upfront payment, this is easy monthly payments - so you can cancel at any time. The only thing I ask is that if you don't like the program at any point - let me know that month, I'll give your money back, but if you stay in the program and take the lessons, it's not fair to everyone else to give your money back for months and months prior, is that fair?

At any point, you can cancel and get your last month's payment back.

You have nothing to lose.

Now, here's the way this is going to work:

It's not going to be $8,000

Or $6,000 like similar training online

Or $4,000 . . .

Instead . . . you can get started for just:

$ 97 a month

with no obligation . . . you can stop anytime you want:

Go Here Now!

www.multiplestreamsmastery.com/startnow

When you enroll, you will get to work with me personally for one full year.

You will receive one new training each week for as long as you remain enrolled (over 50 hours of training each year, delivered weekly)

PLUS - you will get 10 hours of get-started-fast training immediately when you sign up.

AND - you get to talk with me personally for up to 50 hours over the course of the next year.

The full value of all of this, if I were to sell it all separately, is well over $50,000.

AND - it's fully guaranteed, fully refundable if you don't get results <u>when you do what I teach.</u>

Now - I must say this: if you don't do the work, you won't make the money. I am going to give you very specific daily instructions, exactly what to do each day to help you achieve your goals. And of course, as you are selling products and enrolling people in your own coaching program, you will be making money along the way.

How would it feel to work personally with me like this?

How about you?

How would it feel to work with me?

Would it feel good to have someone to get on the phone with when you are stuck on something instead of trying to figure it out on your own?

How would it feel to have someone look at an email, a sales page, a Tele-seminar script and say, change this, change that, so you get it right the first time, so you can make sales fast instead of having to triple split test everything?

How much time would you be able to save by getting it right the first time instead of guessing and trial and error?

How much faster could you achieve your goals by working with someone who's been there done that for 5 years running - and easily on track - ALREADY - to doing it a 6th year? (Instead of guessing??)

So, what about you?

Are you ready?

Are you ready to change your life now - forever (at least on this earth!!)

Excellent - go ahead, sign up now, you will get your first training immediately when you sign up, then we will talk within the next 7 days and begin personalizing the work we do together.

www.multiplestreamsmastery.com/startnow

Now here's the thing: with an offer like this, I can't work with just anyone.

In fact, I don't want to work with everyone.

So, I reserve the right to take this offer down at any time.

And once I get as many clients as I can handle, I will close this offer or raise the price.

If you miss out, you miss out.

I believe this is the opportunity of a lifetime.

This is your year.

This is the year to free you from the ups and downs of the financial system.

This is the year to change your life and free your family.

Let's get started today:

Get started today for just:

$97 a month

www.multiplestreamsmastery.com/startnow

It's Your choice.

I don't want you buying bullet points.

You are buying coaching.

Working with me. Personally

This is personal.

This is going to be about getting YOU to achieve YOUR goals.

The process will vary based on what you know how to do already, how easy it is for you to do each step, and so on.

So, I am going to be coaching you personally on each step of the way to help you achieve your goals.

Not on a bunch of bullet points.

The Program

1) We are going to meet in a very small group atmosphere with about 5 other people who are also going to be building an online information business. Not only will I be working with you personally during that time, you will also get to mastermind and network with

others in the coaching. ($50,000 value)

2) PLUS - you will get-the fast-start training immediately when you sign up.

3) You will get to work with me personally for one full year. (priceless)

4) You will receive one new training each week (over 50 hours of training in the first year, delivered weekly)

5) AND - you get to talk with me online for up to 50 hours over the course of the next year.

6) The full value of all of this, if I were to sell it all separately, is well over $50,000.

OR - if you act today, you can get in for just $97 a month.

AND - it's fully guaranteed, fully refundable if you don't get results when you do what I teach.

Get started now for just $97 a month for personal coaching:

Go to This Link NOW!

www.multiplestreamsmastery.com/startnow

Ok, I know a few of you will want bullet points.

Because you are used to, buying based on bullet points.

They are NOT listed in the order you will learn them.

I will be teaching them to you in the order the YOU NEED THEM.

If you already know something, we will skip it.

Remember - this is personal coaching -

Meaning we are going to work WITH YOU on WHAT YOU NEED - not based on some list of bullet points -

BUT - I know you want them - so here they are:

1) **How to position yourself in your niche** so you are literally perceived as a GURU within 30 days - no matter what your niche is.

2) **My own personal method** of determining EXACTLY which products to create and what people will buy from you

3) **Step by step directions for creating products** in as little as 3-5 hours

4) **My stupid-simple sales letter formula** - I even GIVE you a sample sales letter I wrote for a client - that you can EASILY customize for your niche (I even give you exact directions for that, as well) -so you can write your first sales letter - in just 2-3 hours.

5) **My never-before revealed (except to my highest-level Platinum clients who pay upwards of $12k to work with me) automation formula** for automating in your auto responder every selling email you ever send...and how to make sure buyers don't get sent the same email again, and how to queue up multiple products in

your sales funnel quickly and easily.

6) **My own secret formula for creating one product per week for 8 weeks in a row, so that by the end of 2 months you have 8 products in your sales funnel,** all 8 automatically being promoted to your list based on how long they have been on your list and what they have already bought. How to know if you should REMOVE someone from your email list because they are wasting your time and will probably never buy (did you know I purpose delete as many as 10 - 100 subscribers PER DAY from lists depending on these characteristics?)

7) **My brand new personal formula for creating more time in your day** for the important things, and dropping loser tasks like a hot potato (this is a brand-new teaching, never revealed except to about 30 special clients)

8) **Additionally, I am going to teach you how to put all of this together,** complete with building a list and driving massive traffic - to literally create an automated MACHINE where you literally only must pour traffic in the front end, and sales come out the backend.

In addition, you will learn:

9) **How to create a product funnel in just one month,** complete with 4 products, ranging from $47 on the low end, to $2000 on the high end

10) **How to Determine Precisely What the market will need** in your niche - BEFORE it needs it - so that you can BEAT ALL YOUR COMPETITION to market

11) **Precisely my exact formula for writing a sales letter** from

scratch...without any additional sales letter writing classes or training needed

12) **My own personal never-before-been-revealed outsourcing formula** -where I find my workers, how much I pay them, how I keep them motivated and working their hardest

13) **One more to-be-announced topic** - this will be based on YOUR requests - and these will be evaluated on a first come first served basis AFTER you have enrolled in this class.

In addition to my step by step system for creating an automated system that works like clockwork, and that is easy to implement - and the exact system for automating all this using simple auto-responder techniques (including some hidden techniques many clients have never seen), you are also going to learn:

14) **How to know EXACTLY which products to create** in WHICH order to get the most sales the fastest.

15) **How to create incredible levels of profit from the buyers** on your list (my buy list generates about $15 PER SUBSCRIBER per month).

16) **How to know exactly what to say and write so** that BEFORE someone gets your sales letter they are READY to buy from you

17) **How to correctly manage your time** so that you are focusing on the IMPORTANT things rather than the URGENT (this is my own blended system I personally developed after studying many time management and life management experts...and my clients who have been exposed to this have been BLOWN AWAY)

18) **How to create the precise balance** between building relationship and making sales

19) **Learn the BEST way to create multiple products fast...**in fact, one of my techniques ensures you will have over 50 hours of teaching content in the first year...while simultaneously submitting over 500 articles to ezinearticles...and you don't write a word!

In addition to my step by step system for writing emails that convert - and the exact system for making sales to your email list, you are also going to learn:

20) **How to write subject lines** that force people to open your emails and read them.

21) **How to create incredible levels of response** from the emails you write.

22) **How to create content in your emails** that offer the right balance between value for the lead and getting them to click over to your sales page

23) **How to correctly write/craft/create your emails** so that they consistently create trust and sales.

24) **How to create the precise balance** between content and sales emails to maximize sales to your email list.

25) **Learn the BEST way to build relationships** with your list fast.

I also teach you:

26) **How to use the 7 forms of psychological trust triggers** to bond with your subscribers fast so they continue to open your emails

over time and buy from you when asked.

27) **How to write each of the following types of emails** (exactly what they are and how they are used as well):

credibility email, content emails, gift emails, trust building emails, communication emails, high response emails, re-activation emails, buying emails, selling your product emails, selling affiliate product emails, product launch formula emails

28) **I will teach you each of those types of emails**, exactly how to use them, when to use them in your campaign, and how to write each of those kinds of emails

29) **How to time the delivery of your emails** based on the type of list you have, the niche you are in, and the price point of your product (get this wrong, and sales won't happen)

30) **How to know the precise point** at which you need to change what you are offering to a list, based on their responsiveness

31) **How to easily create a product launch series of emails**

32) **How to use articles and PDFs in your email campaign** to create high levels of credibility and trust - and how to sell through those articles and PDFs (A unique twist in article marketing you probably have never seen exactly quite like this)

33) **Why some types of emails convert well** on some lists but poorly on others - and how to know the difference

34) **How to prepare your subscribers for a new launch** of a product or affiliate product and have people ready to act when the buy button comes out.

35) **Discover my own secret for building tight bonds** with my subscribers so they trust me and not only buy from me, but consistently purchase multiple products (I have some clients who have bought 20, 30...even 40 times from me!) and how you can train your subscribers to do the same thing

36) **3 simple techniques to write your auto-responder campaign**...in fact, an easy way to write a 100 - email auto-responder campaign in a short period of time (if you had a 100-email responsive auto-responder campaign, would that increase your income?)

37) **Step-by-step methods for writing** each individual email

38) **How to create multiple sales funnels** based on what someone's first purchase.

39) **How to create 50 + email campaigns** to sell your products.

40) **How to use advanced website optimization** to optimize the sales conversion rate of each of those products in the campaign. Meaning that if one product converts at 3% and another convert at 1%, then the one converting at 3% is moved to the front of the campaign and the one converting at 1% is moved to the back of the campaign (or taken off the market, or the sales letter re-written, or the sales letter split test until it performs better, at which point it is moved back to a higher point in the campaign.

41) **How to create one hour of new training per week** (that is 50 hours per year, or 250 after 5 years)

42) **How to constantly split test the long-term customer value** based on which squeeze page and traffic source they come in on.

You'll also learn:

43) **How to split test the long run customer** value based on the first product they buy.

44) **How to scientifically optimize the process** for determining what products will sell best to each product, based on what they have bought before.

45) **How to focus on automation, not immediate sales.** This is important. Most people are so concerned with making more sales this week that they don't automate. And if you don't automate, you CANNOT grow past your own limit of efficiency. Can't be done. So, you get stuck, just like you are.

46) **How to run a program of constant marginal improvement** on my sales letters, emails, email campaigns, email funnels, sales funnels, and all other profit-producing activity.

I'm Also Going to Teach You:

47) **How to master a process of time management** that allows me to get more done in 2 hours per day than most people can get done in 10 hours

48) **How I keep my business model and my implementation** of it drastically simple (you cannot personally manage a 3-million-dollar business if you have 1000 different systems to monitor). Because of this, I use very simply processes, very simple software, and advanced sampling techniques rather than tracking ever sale and conversion.49

49) **Many more tips and tricks and techniques and things others might call "secrets"** that will boost your internet sales 1000% when

you implement them

50) **My own personal model for determining what people want** to buy, and in what order the way to buy it

51) **Step by step exactly how to write a complete series of emails** that compels your subscribers to do business with you and not your competition

52) **A super-simple system of creating world-wide credibility** just by creating and publishing easy content online

Here's what you are going to learn:

53) **My foolproof method of positioning yourself as a guru** online fast (30 days)

54) **The exact way to get buyers to come into your list.** If you don't know this, you are probably getting freebie seekers on your list, and they don't buy.

55) **My proven 5-hour product creation method** for creating internet marketing niche trainings fast that sell for between $37 and $97 easy.

56) **My secret source for getting sales letters written** super-fast and that convert well.

57) **How to create a coaching program from scratch** (with my secret method, you don't even have to write the first lesson before your first client pays you) (67 minutes)

58) **How to record your coaching** lessons in such a way that you turn them into long term products

59) **How to outsource your traffic** for cheap in the Philippines like I do

60) **My super easy method for building a list fast**

61) **My own personal method** of getting 15% - 20% CTR at ezinearticles in my sleep

62) **How to let your list tell you what they will buy** before you create anything

63) **How to get people to tell you their coaching needs** before you create the coaching program

64) **The exact formula for writing an eBook** that gets results

PLUS:

You are also going to get:

65) **My own squeeze page template** that is designed for gurus

66) **The one secret way that you will position yourself** as the go-to person for your chosen niche, even if you don't have any experience yet - (without this, you'll struggle to get started)

67) **My own secret formula for making your entire business** - back-of-the-napkin simple

68) **My own $250k formula** for info-product selling

69) **My own formula** for getting people to sign up for coaching without a sales letter

And there's more:

70) **I'm also going to give you my formula** for crafting coaching that is specific to a certain person, recording it, and selling it as training later

71) **My personal method of choosing** article topics that convert

72) **How to use the search engines** to drive you buyers

73) **My own email-writing formula** to get people buying fast once they get on your list

74) **How to Choose the Right Products** for Your Niche, That Your Prospects Really Want to Buy

75) **Exactly how** to create your first $37 product

76) **Exactly how** to create your second $97 product

77) **Exactly how** to create your third $297 product

78) **Exactly how** to launch an entry level coaching program

And I also teach you:

79) **How to easily think up stuff** to teach in your niche

80) **How to easily outline your products** so that they are easy to create

81) **Also - how to easily write an eBook** if you want to add one more product

82) **How to Create a 4-product funnel** in just one month

83) **My own step by step easy method** for easily recording your products fast

And you will learn exactly:

84) **How to** Create your first product in just 3 hours

85) **How to** Create your Second product in just 6 hours

86) **How to** Launch your coaching program with just 5 hours of preparation

87) **Step by step** how to organize your product funnel with the right products in the right order

88) **How to** easily sell your new products online

89) **How to** Become Unbeatable with Backend Automation

90) **Methods of Increasing Profit** Exponentially

91) **Increase sales page conversion rate**

92) **Implement** subscriber acquisition

93) **Implement** a 90-day daily e-newsletter

94) **Create a backend training** at 5 times the price of the initial product

95) **Create a coaching program** at a monthly price equal to 2 times the price of the initial product

96) **Implement a monthly membership** with a price equal to the price of the initial product

97) **Create an additional backend training** at 10 times the price of the initial product

98) **Create a high-level training program** at 100 times the price of the initial product

99) **Increase traffic** from high quality sources

100) **Increase credibility** through writing books and articles

101) **Outsource all tasks** that do not require your involvement

102) **Increase subscriber bonds** through email

103) **Add an upsell path** to every transaction

104) **Partner with non-competing** training providers for additional revenue streams

105) **Create an affiliate program** for additional sales

106) **Create automated buyer relationship** nurturing campaigns

107) **Test everything** for incremental improvement

108) **Target the portion of your market** that has the highest profit potential

109) **Find an angle** your competition isn't and won't use (concept of hidden backend)

110) **Increase prices**

111) **Price Anchor** for Highest Sales

112) **Learn to sell** the dream

113) **Learn to close** based on value not time

114) **Sell based on trust** not persuasion and hype

115) **Discover an Easy Way** to Create a Complete Training to Sell 100% from Interviews with Experts...you don't have to create a word of the training!

116) **My own special method** of using this kind of training to position YOU as the expert...and get to create future products at will using this method

117) **How to determine** what you will teach on to create a complete training in less than 30 days...and sell for up to $497

118) **How to get your subscribers** to PAY YOU to create your products live (I did this once and am STILL making money selling the files!

119) **A super - simple way of creating new products** FAST even if you have less than 100 subscribers!

120) **How to Connect the Dots** on Creating Coaching Training AND Product Creation at the SAME time

121) **How to sell both products** and coaching program clients from the very first month in your information business (Or use this technique to double current sales fast)

122) **How to decide** EXACTLY what your clients want to learn...so they will pay top dollar for it fast

123) **My own proprietary method** of creating one product per month for over 5 years (yes, that's what I did personally, give or take a month or 2 where I created more than one product, and a couple of times skipped because of a month-long vacation)

124) **This Module includes** my own personal time management system - the very same system that has allowed me to be super-productive and do more online than 99% of the rest in 5 years...

125) **I teach you** how to manage your time so that you only work on what's important...and literally learn to let everything else...go....

126) **A lot of training** out there focuses on your time...I focus on my productiveness...and still get to take a lot of time off...I know this Module doesn't sound...exciting...but frankly, I don't want to give away too much of how I do it right on this page, I frankly don't want anyone reverse engineering my system from this page

127) **Why you should focus** on a targeted part of the market- the part that buys (most people don't buy and if you are targeting volume instead of buyers, no wonder you aren't making enough sales)

128) **A real-life example** from a 5-year client on how she found me (very like how MANY people find me - and an interesting example of how to use articles in your email marketing business

129) **I teach you the easiest** coaching model I know of on earth....my core simplicity model that works like this:

130) **The first 10 days** - credibility campaign (this is a special 10-day email campaign to get people on your list to trust you in 10 days or less

131) **The next - a special email series** I teach you how to write - that gets the people who want more from you (read: coaching) to raise their hand and identify themselves

132) **How to get those people** on the phone for a free 20-minute coaching session and how 1 out of 3 who get on the phone with you will buy coaching or buy your training (exact words, what to say and how to say it)

133) **What to do next** (next 10 emails)

134) **What to create** next to sell the most (here's the thing...you know you should be making $2- $5 per month per subscriber on your list, right? If you are not...you need this model!)

135) **This is my COMPLETE** current traffic model - and I don't plan on sharing this anywhere else - because frankly I don't want 1000's of people doing it like I do it -

136) **My email-based** content marketing model (I don't know of ANYONE on earth teaching this)

137) **Why you shouldn't** create beginner level products (this is worth the price of admission alone)

138) **My personal thoughts** on video marketing (this is contrary, trust me)

139) **Trust Based marketing** is based on the idea that people buy based on trust, not sales hype - and I teach you this model here

140) **How to build trust** fast on your list so people buy fast (the biggest problem with many people's lists is subscribers don't buy soon enough and you get bored, or just plain old go out of business

141) **How to write emails** that create trust - frequency, filtering, etc.

142) **How to price** for long term sales (get this wrong, people buy once or not at all, and your advertising dollars are wasted

143) **How to use pricing** psychology to make more sales (I don't know anyone who is teaching this right now - although I think many gurus are doing this, even if they don't even realize it

144) **Why to price** from high to low or low to high

145) **What kinds of products** to create at what price points to create maximum sales

146) **How to filter out** beginners who don't buy and waste your time

147) **Why 90% of your subscribers** don't buy and how to filter through them

148) **Much, much deeper nuanced material** I've never revealed outside of my highest coaching programs

149) **My brand-new content marketing model** (this is article marketing on steroids)

150) **How to leverage yourself 100** - 1000 times

151) (**Note: this is one secret** - my new complete content marketing plan - that I wasn't planning to reveal before I took my business to the covert level with my new marketing launch - but have decided to include this here before I lock things down)

152) **The exact plan** for how to maximize Google and search engine traffic over the long term (instead of one-month fads that disappear

after a few people get results, you don't want to build that kind of business, trust me)

Go ahead - you know this training is worth every cent. . . hundreds of past clients love my training - just do it - get signed up today, let's get you on track today!

Go to This Link:

www.multiplestreamsmastery.com/startnow

Here's A Full List on What's Covered in This

12-Part Multiple Streams Mastery™ Coaching Course

MODULE 1

Multiple Streams of Income Overview

7 Reasons Why You Need to Have Multiple Streams of Income

Multiple Streams Types of Business

How to Build a Mailing List

How to Create Your First Product

How to build and Promote Affiliate Programs

How to Get a Domain Name and Web Hosting

How to Create a Free Offer

How to Offer Bonuses

How to Launch a Product

How to Get an Autoresponder Account (AWeber)

Configuring Your Autoresponder (AWeber)

How to Schedule Your Follow Up Series

MODULE 2

Fixed Term Membership Sites

Why Fixed Term Membership Sites?

How to Build Fixed Term Membership Sites

How to Price Your Membership

How to Build Your First Online Course

How to Structure Your Course

Where to Find Membership Site Content

How to Create Your Subscription Forms

How to Schedule Your Member Email Series

Membership Site Scripts

How to Get Loyal, Paying Members

Membership Site Income Streams

MODULE 3

Online Network Marketing

Why Online Network Marketing?

Social Media Methods, Tricks and Shortcuts

Pros and Cons of Network Marketing

How to Attract Joint Venture opportunities

How to Attract Affiliate opportunities

How to Promote efficiently and effectively

How to Create Lead Capture Pages

How to Build Your Email List Fast

How to Generate Qualified Leads

How to Systemize Your Business

MODULE 4

Traffic Generation

Facebook Ads

Facebook Groups

Facebook Closed Communities

Solo Ads

Google Ad words

Social Media Sites Advertising

Blogging

...AND MORE!

REMEMBER –

"THE MORE ACTION YOU CAN TAKE, THE MORE MONEY YOU CAN MAKE"

- DR. MARK ZUPO

12-Step-by-step Dynamic Modules packed with valuable propriatory Self-paced Multiple Streams Training.

Audio and video training for everyone to learn while engaged in other activities

The 1-Million Dollar total concept book that launched a Mastery Revolution™

Appendix 1

Resources

People I Follow

Alex Mandossian	-	Master of Virtual Marketing
Amy Porterfield	-	Webinars that Convert
Brendon Bruchard	-	Master of Expert's Academy
Andy Jenkins	-	Webinar Marketing
Anik Singal	-	Lurn, Inc.
Armand Morin	-	Internet Marketing
Christiana Hill	-	Success Coach
David S. Garland	-	Online Webinars
Derek Halpern	-	7-Figure Courses
Dori Clark	-	The Expert Toolkit
Dr. Mark Zupo	-	Multi Streams Mastery
Frank Kern	-	Master of Sales Pitch Funnel
James Wedmore	-	Video Marketing
Jay Fiset	-	Masterminds

Jeff Herring	-	Profitable Lifestyles
Jeff Walker	-	The Launch Formula
Jim Edwards	-	Internet Marketing
John L Dumas	-	Podcasting
Liz Tomey	-	IM Services
Mari Smith	-	Facebook Marketing
Mark Harbert	-	Video Marketing
Mike Filsaime	-	Online Marketing
Mike Koenigs	-	Traffic Generation
Mike Stewart	-	Internet Audio Guy
Russell Brunson	-	DotCom Funnels
Ryan Deiss	-	Digital Marketing
Seam Mize	-	Coaching Programs
Selena Soo	-	Impacting Millions
Tom Antion	-	Internet Marketing
Tony Robbins	-	Life Coach
Yaro Starak	-	Blog Marketing

Appendix 2

Internet Business Tools I Use

Actionetics	Easy VSL	Presenter Media
Amazon Create Space	Facebook	Rent-A-Coder
BackPack	Facebook Live	Rev.com
Bing Ads	Pexel	Script Engage
Buzzfeed	Google Ads	Soundcloud
Buzzsumo	Google Drive	Sound Forge
Camtasia	Grasshopper	Square Register
Canva	Hootsuite	Stripe
ClickBank	Infusionsoft	Survey Monkey
ClickFunnels	Instagram	Thrive Themes
Designrr	JVZoo	Thunderclap
Edgar	Leadpages	Twitter
Easy Sketch Pro	Mail Chimp	Webinar Jeo
Easy Video Suite	Manychat	Youtube

Upcoming Projects

BookKamp™

The world's first 3-Day Self-publishing BookKamp™ for aspiring entrepreneurs and writers looking to help boost their online presence, build credibility and authority.

MPI™

The Passive-Profits Mastery Program™ for aspiring entrepreneurs to build a brand and a business that is recognized immediately.

Appendix 3

Systems

1. **Production System**

- Product creation
- Product repurposes
- Product hierarchy

2. **Breakthrough System**

- Social Media Presence*
- Your Book!
- Your Brand
- Your Expertise
- Your Launch
- Your Mission

3. **Connection System**

- Your Blog*Your Website*
- Social Media Accounts*
- Your Podcast

4. **Engagement System**

- Webinars
- Seminars
- Sales Funnels*
- Facebook Communities

5. Delivery System

- eMail Marketing*
- Networking
- Affiliates

6. Automation system

- Affiliates*
- Private Facebook Page
- Group Facebook Page*

7. Relationship System

- Online Presence*
- Personal Coaching
- Yearly Mastermind
- Yearly Event
- Subordinate Mentors [A Biggie to Come!]

8. **Support system**

- Affiliates*
- Private Facebook Page
- Group Facebook Page*

* Many systems can be on autopilot and operate with little behind the scenes support and maintenance.

Legal Stuff: Lawyers – you know….

Disclaimer: We do NOT believe in get rich quick programs. We believe in individual effort, adding value and dedication to reach your goals. It's a fact that one who does not act will see no results whatsoever. The results featured on this document are not the norm and are extraordinary results from hard work, commitment and dedication by following through and acting. You will get no results whatsoever if you assume success by soaking up information products, joining program after program expecting that your life will change with instant riches. If this is how you think or what you expect, this is not for you. Your results are based upon your ACTIONS, ENERGY, INTEREST, INVESTMENT, INTELLECT, EXPERIENCE, COMMITTMENT, TRAINING, EDUCATION AND MORE! If you want a magic button that will fulfill your life with riches, then please leave this page and do NOT purchase. Our products are intended to help you share your message with the world while growing your business. It is educational only. It is not legal or business advice. We don't make any guarantees about your own results because we don't know you. You might be the smartest person in the room or the dumbest person or woman ever. Results in life are solely based on decisions made. We are here to help and guide you to move forward faster by giving you awesome content, direction and strategies to reach your end goal. There are no guarantees in life or business. Please check the content thoroughly on this page and that you are committed to taking relentless action and will put in the effort before you decide to make a purchase. If not, then please leave this page and do not purchase. This product / training / information does not guarantee income or success, and examples of the product owner's and other person's results do not represent an indication of future success or earnings. Please don't interpret any of this presentation as some sort of promise or implication of your future earnings. My results aren't even remotely typical. There is nothing simple about Internet Marketing in any form. I've been at this for 21 years, and naturally have a bit of an advantage as a result. The average person who buys any "business building" course (or something similar) rarely gets any results at all for many reasons. Kind of like how the average person who buys home exercise equipment rarely ends up looking like the person in the commercials. I don't know why that is, but I think it's safe to say it's true across the board. THIS ENDEAVOR IS ALL HARD. And it takes **WORK, EFFORT, TRAINING, COMMITMENT, INGENUITY, FORESIGHT, HINDSIGHT and RISK!**

* My / Our results are A-TYPICAL, (NOT TYPICAL), because we are a-typical people and we work our asses off day and night. That's why you probably won't have the same results as us. We cannot promise that you'll even have similar results because we don't know if you will work as hard as us. Your success in business (and in life) depends on YOU, your aptitude, your ability, your skills, your work ethic, and many other factors out of our control. Your individual success does NOT depend on us or on this product. Please read over all the legal pages below before buying. The information contained in this presentation and product is for education -- purposes only. This is information designed to help you understand the specific information covered. It is not an attempt to render tax, legal, or business advice. This is not a business opportunity. How you use the information is entirely up to you. While every effort has been made to accurately represent the information along with our opinions and insights, any claims made, or examples given, although believed to be accurate, should not be relied on in any way in deciding whether to purchase. IMPORTANT: ALWAYS do your OWN due-diligence before making any purchases, whether we recommend them or not.

Never, EVER purchase anything that you cannot afford. Avoid purchasing products that promise ridiculous results, like "Getting Rich Quick" or ridiculous promises. If it sounds odd, then it probably is! Most people don't do anything with the products they buy, and most of the time, their results are zero, just like your gym membership, right? No, there is no such thing as a "Free Lunch". Don't do drugs, stay in school, keep your nose clean and listen to your Mother.

"When I am asked, "What do I do?",
I respond by saying, Everything I can."
- Dr. Mark Zupo

"I deliver people's Destiny on
Demand when I teach them
how to achieve their personal
success and self-empowerment
from their own efforts."
"Which one do you want
to hear about first?"

- Dr. Mark Zupo

ABOUT THE AUTHOR

Dr. Mark Zupo is a dynamic top-selling author of several books on leadership and he is a leader in digital technology marketing in Atlanta, Georgia. His career spans more than 30 years of technical management, business and academic disciplines. Dr. Mark's relationship-building human factors and engagement skills are essential to an Internet Marketing and Relationship-building persona. Mark has championed his academic career as a leadership influencer and innovator.

Google Mark Zupo for more.

"I don't want to spend the last days of my life accepting regret for the thing I haven't done, the shots I didn't take or the opportunities I've had that were passed by. I live to help other people with their self-development and dreams for success. It's not about how much money one makes...it's about what you do with the money after you make it. I am open to coaching others to find their success. That's my success."

Dr. Mark Zupo

Podcast, Blog, and Media...Interview Opportunities upon Request
Go to: InterviewDrMarkZupo

7 Money No's

I'm bad with money.

Money doesn't grow on trees.

Only the rich get richer.

Money corrupts people.

Rich people are evil.

Money is hard to come by.

Money is the root of all evil!

...If you believe any of this, I have several thousand acres east of Fort Lauderdale up for sale. Let's talk.

"Today's mess,
tomorrow's success."
- Dr. Mark Zupo

Success2Squared™

Business-Building Diagrams™

*<u>*Restricted to Platinum coaching members only</u>*

1. Process
2. Visibility
3. Systems
4. Value Proposition
5. Foundation
6. Listbuilding
7. Launch
8. Fears
9. Needs –Wants - Desires
10. Patterns
11. V.I.P. - Valuable, Irresistible, Profitable
12. PASS - Problem, Agitate, Story, Solution
13. TIB - Trust, Imagine, Benefit
14. GAS - Guarantee, Audience, Social Proof
15. CCC - Call to Act, Accept, Action

Flow Charts

**Restricted to Platinum coaching members only.*

My personal LAUNCH SUCCESS flowchart

My personal SALES FUNNEL flowchart

My personal WEBINAR flowchart

My personal MEMBERSHIP flowchart

My personal SOCIAL MEDIA flowchart

My personal BUSINESS MINDMAP flowchart

My personal MASTER COACHING flowchart

My personal ONLINE MARKETING flowchart

Notes
Part 1

1. Recognize your desire to be an entrepreneur
2. Maintain your enthusiasm but be open to learn from other's experience, successes and failures.
3. Don't be afraid to fail to consider a failure a lesson.
4. Approach your entrepreneurship logically.
5. Determine where you want to be and work backwards to determine the steps needed to get there.
6. Determine how much you want to make monthly and annually and reverse engineer the daily, weekly and monthly goals to get there.
7. Define every transaction to the penny and then "rinse and repeat" to scale it up.
8. Determine how many daily, weekly and monthly transaction you will need to meet your goal.
9. Never Quit!
10. NEVER QUIT!

Notes

1. Strategize everything. Plan and do. Do it again better. Never quit. Plan, decide and act.

2. GET A MENTOR! Think, Strategize, Plan, Try, Do, Do-Again, And-Again, Keep on Doing and Expect Success!

3. Stop doing what you hate and start doing what you love. The money will follow.

"Sooner or later, the man who learns from his failures will be the one sought after for his guidance, counsel and formula on how to be successful in the endeavors of life."

- Ogwo David Emenike

Notes

Made in the USA
Monee, IL
04 November 2026

67387216R00144